BRÈVES DE SAISON

HAÏKUS

François-Bernard Tremblay

BRÈVES DE SAISON

accompagné des encres
de Brigitte Sladek

Préface de Serge Tomé

Les Éditions
David

62476633/

Les Éditions David remercient de leur appui :
le Conseil des Arts du Canada,
le ministère du Patrimoine canadien,
par l'entremise du Partenariat interministériel
avec les communautés de langue officielle (PICLO),
le Secteur franco-ontarien du Conseil des arts de l'Ontario
et la Ville d'Ottawa.

Elles remercient également :
Alexandra et Patrick Champagne, Coughlin & Associés Ltée,
le Cabinet juridique Emond Harnden,
la Firme comptable Vaillancourt ◆ Lavigne ◆ Ashman.

Données de catalogage avant publication (Canada)

Tremblay, François-Bernard, 1970-
    Brèves de saison / François-Bernard Tremblay ;
accompagné des encres de Brigitte Sladek.

(Voix intérieures - haïku)

ISBN 2-922109-98-4

    I. Titre. II. Collection.

PS8589.R417B74 2003   C841'.6   C2003-902992-1

Maquette de la couverture : Pierre Bertrand
Illustrations : Brigitte Sladek
Mise en pages et montage : Lynne Mackay

Les Éditions David, 2003
1678, rue Sansonnet
Ottawa (Ontario) K1C 5Y7

Téléphone : (613) 830-3336
Télécopieur : (613) 830-2819

Courriel : ed.david@sympatico.ca
Internet : www3.sympatico. ca/ed. david/

PS
8589
.R44386
B74
2003

Le Conseil des Arts | The Canada Council
du Canada | for the Arts

ONTARIO ARTS COUNCIL
CONSEIL DES ARTS DE L'ONTARIO

Ottawa

À Nathalie
À Audréane

Un cri dans la nuit
Épouvante ou fulgurance
La faim d'Audréane

Élie DUVIVIER

PRÉFACE

rutilante décapotable
je ne suis pas jaloux
il pleut à boire debout

premières lueurs
sur la route cette nuit
les yeux du renard roux

Lorsque François-Bernard Tremblay m'a demandé d'écrire la préface de son recueil, j'ai immédiatement accepté… J'avais en mémoire ces haïkus. Alors je me suis dit : « je vais être en bonne compagnie. C'est un homme qui a le regard large et la parole libre. » Pas de haïku sincère sans cette liberté intérieure qui permet de poser sur les choses un regard détendu, à la fois distant et attentif, et de noter sereinement tous ces petits instants qui constituent une vie.

Car le haïku, c'est pour moi, d'abord le regard.

> *deux grosses fraises*
> *sur le costume de ma fille*
> *l'une cousue, l'autre écrasée*

Lorsque l'on pratique le haïku assidûment, notre regard sur les choses se modifie. Nous percevons davantage les relations d'associations symboliques, enchaînements, proximités sémantiques, mises en rapport… Elles agissent par des renforcements, complémentarités, oppositions, effets d'échelle, jeux de mots, ironie… Le monde devient alors un jeu pour l'œil qui débusque sans effort toute cette « architecture projetée » qui trouve sa source dans notre vécu, mais aussi dans tous les modèles de notre conscient et inconscient.

> *mort précoce*
> *l'éphémère*
> *mangé par la truite*

l'électricité
revenue depuis plus d'une heure
un couple s'embrasse à la chandelle

Le haïku, ce n'est pas toujours sérieux… Cette affirmation est sacrilège pour beaucoup de théoriciens qui vident le haïku de sa substance en en faisant une poésie compassée, très formelle et plutôt « fleur bleue ». Si le haïku avait été sérieux, aurait-il survécu? Il passe et devient même pour plusieurs une poésie « zen », intellectuellement construite en respectant tout un jeu de règles très précis mais très fluide… Rien de pire qu'une poésie conventionnelle, vide d'émotion. On oublie trop son caractère légèrement moqueur qui s'exprime le plus souvent dans la mise en rapport humoristique des choses. Ce recueil en présente une grande variété.

le cadavre de mon frère
sur la table basse
une bière pleine

né la veille
l'éphémère
agonise

Le haïku est réservé à l'observation objective des moments agréables de ce qui nous entoure... Oui, pour certains, mais ce n'est pas exact à mon sens. Le haïku, c'est la vie. Avec ses hauts et ses bas. Lorsqu'on le maîtrise, le haïku s'écrit naturellement, en toutes circonstances. Il parle alors de tout et on lui reproche souvent de s'approcher de sa forme voisine, le senryu, marqué par l'implication du lecteur au niveau des sentiments explicitement exprimés. Il existe cependant une écriture du haïku qui exprime implicitement nos sentiments, nos peurs, nos inquiétudes, nos joies, nos amours, notre affection. Son écriture est aussi parfois une chose à laquelle on se raccroche dans des situations de détresse profonde.

les femmes et la bière
rousses, blondes, vertes
soir de Saint-Patrick

tison ardent
dans la nuit de juillet
la luciole

Le haïku, c'est l'insertion dans le Cosmos. Pas de haïku sans un lien à ce qui est le fruit de nos perceptions, à cet univers dont nous ne sommes qu'une partie infime. Sans lequel nous n'avons pas d'existence. Il faut prendre le mot « Cosmos » au sens métaphysique. C'est tout ce qui est perçu, saisi par nos sens et qui forme en nous une représentation mentale de ce qui nous entoure. C'est aussi une incursion dans le Temps où la vie est jalonnée de repères affectifs (décès, anniversaires, réjouissances) ou collectifs (événements). Cette insertion dans le Temps (incluant la météo) est essentielle à mon sens, car elle pose un ancrage dans notre histoire personnelle ainsi que dans celle du lecteur qui, au travers d'un détail, est mis en situation. Chacun vit le Temps et donc s'approprie facilement ce qui le jalonne.

au petit matin
parfum d'hydrangée dans l'air
neige à ma fenêtre

Pas de haïku sans référence aux sens. Le monde nous parvient au travers de nos perceptions sensorielles. Le reste est pure construction intellectuelle. Le haïku est la plus petite forme « poétique ». Pour la rendre efficace, il faut y insérer des traits forts. Et quoi de plus fort que ces sensations sous-jacentes au langage exprimé? Elles se raccrochent au vécu du lecteur et utilisent alors le souvenir de ses propres sensations. D'ailleurs, nos souvenirs s'ancrent dans notre mémoire au travers des sensations perçues. Donc, pas de haïku sans sensation. Un haïku sincère, sur le moment, c'est souvent une notation, qui contient tout ce qui est dans notre entourage, toutes nos perceptions, toutes les images mentales du conscient et de l'inconscient, actives à ce moment. C'est tout cela qui est en filigrane dans un bon haïku.

Le haïku est une démarche. On commence par écrire, en respectant les règles nombreuses et contradictoires… du « figé », du « construit ». Puis peu à peu, l'écriture se fait automatique, plus libre, le regard s'épure, s'ouvre. Le haïku devient le compagnon de tous les moments.

En lisant le recueil de François-Bernard Tremblay, j'ai été émerveillé par la diversité des sujets qu'il aborde et par la largeur de la palette des sentiments implicitement exprimés. Un recueil, c'est comme un album photo. Il permet de voir le monde par les yeux de l'auteur, de partager avec lui ce que sont ses émotions intimes, sa vie de tous les jours. Et celui-ci est un bien beau recueil.

Serge TOMÉ

Saisons chaudes

Quand elle fond
La glace avec l'eau
Se raccommode

Matsunaga TEITOKU

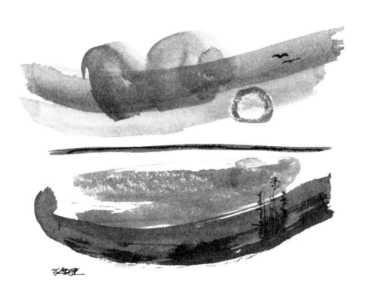

BRIGITTE SLADEK, *sans titre*, encre

solstice d'été
éternelle question
avancer ou reculer l'heure ?

jouant avec une marguerite
elle m'aime passionnément,
        à la folie, pas du tout...
la marmotte

tison ardent
dans la nuit de juillet
la luciole

premières lueurs
sur la route cette nuit
les yeux du renard roux

né la veille
l'éphémère
agonise

à tant chanter
la cigale devra visiter
la fourmi sa voisine

va-t-il pleuvoir?
il est enrhumé
le cri du huard

soleil de juillet
délaissé par la meute
le traîneau à chiens

regarder la surface de l'eau
en dessous
un autre monde

voir Les Grands Explorateurs
observer le monde
par les yeux d'un autre

après l'amour
la flamme dans tes yeux
l'âtre gémit

cette nuit à tes côtés
au réveil trouver ton billet
adieu

surprise au bistro
cette jolie femme accoudée au bar
mon voisin

androgyne à ma table hier
le serveur la serveuse
impossible de trancher

armés de détecteurs
les jeunes pirates de la plage
font fortune

mer, soleil, bikinis
de retour chez moi
un coquillage dans le caleçon

Brigitte Sladek, *sans titre*, encre

vie sale et ingrate
le poète Vanier est mort
anonyme

allongé dans le parc
brin d'herbe et poésie
entre les dents

danse de Geisha
santal et fleur d'oranger
dans ses parfums

nos parfums subtils
et ma transe soudaine
intime fragrance

levé tôt ce matin
déjeuné avec ma fille
revenant de sa soirée

sourire de la mère
devant l'impatience de sa fille
héritage du père

des cris
la chouette de Riopelle
sur la toile

                    entre mes mains
                    le manuscrit de toute une vie
                    amour et règlements de compte

le chef gesticule
au-dessus du buffet
des mouches

je ferme les yeux
l'odeur du pain
devant cette confiserie

au large de jeunes phoques
s'offrent un joyeux festin
sushi sous-marin

histoire de pêche
à les entendre ils en ont pris...
plusieurs caisses

la cabane d'oiseau
envahie par les écureuils
crise du logement

virevoltes
il a l'air d'un gros taon
le bébé colibri

le béluga
venu nous voir près du quai
à la une des quotidiens

mort précoce
l'éphémère
mangé par la truite

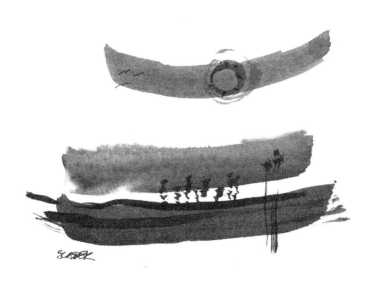

Brigitte Sladek, *sans titre*, encre

la musique s'achève
du bout des doigts
pianoter d'ennui

sortie de son lit
elle emprunte le mien
la rivière ce matin

les femmes et la bière
rousses, blondes, vertes
soir de Saint-Patrick

éclairs, coups de tonnerre
ça gronde aussi
chez les voisins d'en bas

dans la cour d'école
deux gamins se disputent...
qui aura le cœur de la fillette?

deux grosses fraises
sur le costume de ma fille
l'une cousue, l'autre écrasée

étendue au soleil
une brise la caresse
mon regard aussi

nouvelle saison
rendez-vous doux
et pluie fraîche

Saisons froides

J'y suis résolu :
Je vais de ce pas m'enrhumer
Pour voir la neige

Sugiyama Sampû

Brigitte Sladek, *sans titre*, encre

au petit matin
parfum d'hydrangée dans l'air
neige à ma fenêtre

insomnie cette nuit d'hiver
par le carreau, la pleine lune
envie soudaine d'un fromage

ratissage automnal
la brise éparpille les feuilles
ratissage automnal

sur le lac
rides et pattes d'oie
mon visage

sur le trottoir d'en face
femme enceinte glacée par le froid
bébé bien au chaud

au coin d'une ruelle
ballon abandonné par des gosses
empreintes dans la neige

voie maritime
de ma cabine
pleine lune d'octobre

le fjord en hiver
ah! flâner jusqu'au printemps
bien au chaud

au cimetière
sur une dalle de pierre
une veuve noire

soirée au coin du feu
mon chien fait le mort
le Canadien prend les devants

début avril
déjà sortis
les perce-neige

des chants dans le ciel
et une figure géométrique
des outardes

brise hivernale
la porte bat au vent
les gosses ne referment jamais

l'électricité
revenue depuis plus d'une heure
un couple s'embrasse à la chandelle

le vent plaintif
toute cette nuit durant
m'a soufflé ces mots

chalet au Nord
dans ma bouche
le sucré de ta peau

Brigitte Sladek, *sans titre*, encre

retour du soleil
des rires d'enfants
après la neige

la surprise de ma fille
à sa première cuillerée
de gaspacho

le cadavre de mon frère
sur la table basse
une bière pleine

devant le tombeau fermé
le sourire sur les visages
des femmes de sa vie

Inuit du Nord
dans ton sourire
un peu d'Asie

sculptures et tableaux
musée à ciel ouvert
archipel de Mingan

panne électrique
à l'ombre du barrage...
Baie-Comeau

plaquebières
que d'exotisme
dans l'Ungava

ici dans la toundra
entre chien et loup
prend tout son sens

Nunavut
deux mondes
verdure et givre

Paris sous la neige
autos tamponneuses dans les rues
si j'avais les ailes d'un ange,
            je partirais pour...

                        rutilante décapotable
                        je ne suis pas jaloux
                        il pleut à boire debout

violente bourrasque
sur la branche
une feuille résiste

blanche giboulée d'octobre
je peux suivre le gibier
à la trace

du pommier
un fruit tombe sur ma tête
j'invente ce haïku

mise en abyme
la tête dégarnie de Lafleur
sur la patinoire

Brigitte Sladek, *sans titre*, encre

corne de brume
et chant du navire
fjord d'octobre

Longue-Rive
promenade sur la grève
retour des oies sauvages

14 avril
naviguer parmi les glaciers bleus
le Titanic en mémoire

sculpté par le vent, l'eau salée
et des années d'intempéries
le visage de cet Inuit

recouverte de neige
au milieu de l'erreur boréale
une épinette

basse saison
déserté des touristes
l'hôtel pour moi seul

matin de tempête
des envies de partir... de rester
la voiture refuse de démarrer

solstice d'hiver
le rire gras d'un père Noël
qui attend Nez rouge

BRIGITTE SLADEK

Brigitte Sladek est née à Hambourg, en Allemagne, en 1954 ; au Québec depuis 1992, elle a vécu sept ans à Moisie, sur la Côte-Nord.

Différents voyages d'étude à travers l'Europe, les États-Unis, le Canada ainsi qu'un séjour de six ans au Rwanda ont fortement marqué sa peinture. On peut reconnaître, dans son style, l'influence de l'art africain ainsi que celle de la présence autochtone en Amérique du Nord ; ces influences se manifestent tant dans les formes, les couleurs, les textures que dans les thèmes choisis. Toute son œuvre est l'expression d'une quête spirituelle authentique.

Brigitte Sladek a commencé à peindre en 1969 et s'y consacre à temps complet depuis 1990. Elle a participé à de multiples événements culturels et plusieurs de ses œuvres font partie de collections privées tant au Québec, en Suisse, en Australie qu'en Allemagne. Aux Éditions David, elle a contribué aux illustrations de *Dire le Nord*, paru en 2002.

Table des matières

Préface   9

Saisons chaudes   17

Saisons froides   45

Brigitte Sladek   74

Illustrations

Encres de Brigitte Sladek

Déjà parus dans la collection
« Voix intérieures – Haïku »

Collection dirigée par Francine Chicoine

BEAUDRY, Micheline et Jean DORVAL, *Blanche mémoire*, Ottawa, 2002.

BANNINO, Vanessa-S.-E., *Souffle de paix*, Ottawa, 2002.

Chevaucher la lune, sous la direction d'André DUHAIME (Préface de Maurice Coyaud), Ottawa, 2001.

CHICOINE, Francine et Jeanne PAINCHAUD, *Sous nos pas* (Préface de Michel Garneau), Ottawa, 2003.

Dire la faune, sous la direction de Francine CHICOINE (Préface de Robert Melançon), Ottawa, 2003.

Dire le Nord, sous la codirection de Francine CHICOINE et André DUHAIME (Préface de Marc Pelletier), Ottawa, 2002.

DUHAIME, André, *Cet autre rendez-vous* (Préface de Robert Melançon), Orléans, 1996, 2ᵉ tirage (1999).

DUHAIME, André et Gordan ŠKILJEVIĆ, *Quelques jours en hiver et au printemps*, Orléans, 1997.

DUHAIME, André et Carol LEBEL, *De l'un à l'autre*, Orléans, 1999.

Éphémère, ouvrage collectif, Ottawa, 2002.

FAUQUET, Ginette, *Ikebana*, Ottawa, 2002.

GAUTHIER, Jacques, *Pêcher l'ombre*, Ottawa, 2002.

Haïku sans frontières : une anthologie mondiale, sous la direction d'André DUHAIME (Préfaces d'Alain Kervern et de Ryu Yotsuya), Orléans, 1998, 2ᵉ tirage (2001).

Haïku et francophonie canadienne, sous la direction d'André DUHAIME, Orléans, 2000.

LEBEL, Carol, *Clapotis du temps,* Ottawa, 2003.

NAYET, Bertrand, *Juste un grand vent* (Préface d'André Duhaime), Ottawa, 2003.

PAINCHAUD, Jeanne, *Soudain*, Ottawa, 2002.

PARADIS, Monique, *Étincelles*, Ottawa, 2002.

PARENT, Monique, *Fragiles et nus*, Ottawa, 2003.

RAIMBAULT, Alain, *Mon île muette*, Ottawa, 2001.

RAIMBAULT, Alain, *New York loin des mers*, Ottawa, 2002.

Rêves de plumes, ouvrage collectif, Ottawa, 2001.

Saisir l'instant, ouvrage collectif, Orléans, 2000.

TREMBLAY, François-Bernard, *Brèves de saison*, (Préface de Serge Tomé), Ottawa, 2003.

TREMBLAY, Jessica, *Le sourire de l'épouvantail*, Ottawa, 2003.

VOLDENG, Évelyne, *Haïkus de mes cinq saisons*, Ottawa, 2001.

Achevé d'imprimer
en août 2003
sur les presses de l'imprimerie AGMV-Marquis
Cap-Saint-Ignace (Québec)
Canada

Women in Management and Life Cycle

Also by Alicia E. Kaufmann

CONSTRUIR EQUIPOS DE TRABAJO EN LA ERA DE LA CONEXIÓN (*with M. De Prado*). Prólogue by Amparo Moraleda. President of IBM.Madrid, Edited by Caja Madrid and University of Alcalá. 2003.

LIDER GLOBAL EN LA VIDA Y EN LA EMPRESA. Madrid, University of de Alcalá, 1999.

TRABAJANDO CON LOS MAYORES (*with R. Frías and Miguel Ángel Sánchez*). Madrid, CIS, 1997.

ORGANIZACIÓN HOTELERA: INNOVACIÓN Y FORMACIÓN. Madrid, Ciencias de la Dirección, 1996.

EL PODER DE LAS ORGANIZACIONES. Madrid, ESIC y Universidad de Alcalá, 2ª edición, 1995. (Power of Organizations, supervised by Charles Perrow, Yale University)

LA GESTIÓN DE LAS RESIDENCIAS DE LA TERCERA EDAD (*with R. Frías and R. Benatar*). Bilbao, Deusto, 1993.

LA ENFERMEDAD GRAVE: ASPECTOS MÉDICO SOCIALES (*with P. Aiach and R. Waissman*). Madrid, Interamericana, McGraw Hill, 1990.

VIVRE UNA MALADIE GRAVE (*with Pierre Aïach and Renée Waissman*). París, Meridiens Klienseck, 1989.

"El suicidio", en DICCIONARIO DE SOCIOLOGÍA de Juan González Anleo (adaptación española). Madrid, Ediciones Paulinas, 1986.

LA LEPRA Y SUS IMÁGENES: ENFERMEDAD ESTIGMÁTICA Y MUERTE SOCIAL. Madrid, Ministerio de Trabajo y Seguridad Social, 1985.

CÁNCER Y SOCIEDAD. Madrid, Mezquita, 1984.

THE SOCIAL DIMENSION OF LEPROSY. Londres, Ilep, 1982.

MARGINACIÓN, PREJUICIO Y ENFERMEDAD. Barcelona, Ciba Geigy, 1981.

Women in Management and Life Cycle

Aspects that Limit or Promote Getting to the Top

Alicia E. Kaufmann
Professor of Sociology of Organizations at Universidad de Alcalá de Henares
Doctorate in Sociology, École des Hautes Études en Sciences Sociales,
Paris and Universidad Complutense, Madrid

Translated by Susana Urra

Foreword by Constanza Tobío

First published in Spanish 2007
English translation published 2008 by
PALGRAVE MACMILLAN
Houndmills, Basingstoke, Hampshire RG21 6XS and
175 Fifth Avenue, New York, N.Y. 10010
Companies and representatives throughout the world

PALGRAVE MACMILLAN is the global academic imprint of the Palgrave
Macmillan division of St. Martin's Press, LLC and of Palgrave Macmillan Ltd.
Macmillan® is a registered trademark in the United States, United Kingdom
and other countries. Palgrave is a registered trademark in the European
Union and other countries.

ISBN-13: 978–0–230–20299–3   hardback
ISBN-10: 0–230–20299–3   hardback

This book is printed on paper suitable for recycling and made from fully
managed and sustained forest sources. Logging, pulping and manufacturing
processes are expected to conform to the environmental regulations of the
country of origin.

A catalogue record for this book is available from the British Library.

A catalogue record for this book is available from the Library of Congress.

10   9   8   7   6   5   4   3   2   1
17   16   15   14   13   12   11   10   09   08

Printed and bound in Great Britain by
CPI Antony Rowe, Chippenham and Eastbourne

Contents

List of Tables   vii

List of Figures   viii

Acknowledgments   ix

Foreword   xi

Author's Biography   xvi

1 Introduction, Goals and Approach   1

2 Background   7
   Existing literature   7
   Film records   10

3 Methodology   13

4 Characteristics of 21st Century Organizations   17
   Analysis of the technological environment   17
   Analysis of the organizational environment   18

5 Identity Dimensions: Women Managers and Motherhood   23
   Identity dimensions   23
   Differences in identity by gender   27
   Identity and the crossroads of motherhood   31
   Taking the drama out of motherhood   36

6 Life Cycle and Types of Women Managers   41
   Theories on the life cycle   41
   Types of women managers: the competitive manager   42
   The integrated manager   55
   The proactive and reactive manager   64
   Life cycle and gender differences   72

7 A Man's Viewpoint: You Want to be Like Goddesses   81
   How they see themselves   81
   How they see women managers   87

8 The Cinderella Complex Versus Financial Freedom   **101**
   Financial socialization as a barrier or a springboard   101
   Money, life cycle and family mandates   105
   Ambition, fear, guilt: values and inhibitions   113

9 Conclusion   **129**
   General concepts and basic concepts   129
   The female perspective   132
   The male perspective   143

Appendix   **149**
Outline for group discussions   149
Outline for in-depth interviews   150

Notes   159

Bibliography   165

Index   169

List of Tables

4.1	Characteristics of the Technological and Organizational Environment	19
4.2	The Company Both Contains and Creates Anxiety	21
5.1	Dimensions of Identity	27
5.2	Differences in Identity According to Gender	31
6.1	Mother-Daughter Bonds	54
6.2	Emotional Maturity Continuum	64
8.1	Spaniards, Money and Happiness	104
8.2	Spaniards and Causes of Unhappiness	104
8.3	Fantasies Linked to Happiness	105
8.4	Financial Socialization and Life Cycle	113
8.5	Traits of a Transformational Leadership	118
8.6	Production Eras and Work Relations	120

List of Figures

A.1   Theories about Women in Management   153
A.2   Gender Identity Differences   153
A.3   Analysis Results Chart – Arguments of Women   154
      Managers and Life Cycle I
A.4   Analysis Results Chart – Arguments of Women   154
      Managers and Life Cycle II
A.5   Analysis Results Chart – Arguments of Women   155
      Managers and Life Cycle III
A.6   Content Analysis of Discourses. Conflict Between   155
      Altruism and Selfishness
A.7   Analysis Results – Female Managers and Money   156
A.8   Analysis Results – Female Managers and Motherhood   156
A.9   Types of Male Arguments   157
A.10 Male Arguments and Attitudes Towards Women's   157
      Development
A.11 Male Arguments and Attitudes Towards Women   158
      Managers

Acknowledgments

I would like to express my gratitude to the President of Centro de Investigaciones Sociológicas, Fernando Vallespín Oña, for trusting me to carry out this study. I would also like to extend a warm acknowledgement to Angel P. Muñoz Regidor, who took the necessary steps to make it happen, and Teresa Peña Gamarra for getting it published.

My thanks go out to the team of people who participated in the initial debates and in designing the various stages of the research work: **Alejandro Swiec, Manuel Zúñiga, María Cuesta Azofra, Paula López and María Eugenia de la Cruz**.

A special thanks to María Jesús Pablos, executive director of the Commission for Cultural, Educational and Scientific Exchange between Spain and the United States, who not only gave up some of her precious time to take part in the discussion groups, but also allowed us to use Commission rooms for the group discussions.

Without a doubt, the main characters in this study are all the managers – men and women – who took time out from their work and leisure hours to participate through in-depth interviews and group discussions. I am therefore grateful to Sara Neira, María Benjumea, Pilar Cardenal, Raquel Pérez, Almudena Rodríguez Tarodo, Claire Benatar, Carmen Vela, Mercedes Pescador, Mercedes Perrier, Julieta Ballart, Eva Levy, Ana María Llopis, Celia de Anca, Elena Gil, Daisy Escobar, Marianne Thomsen, Pino Bethencourt, Yanire Braña, Cristina Díaz, Carmen Daniel, Rebecca Finger, Regina Revilla and María Luis Ramírez de Arellano, as well as to male managers such as José Manuel Casado, Juan José Almagro, Iván Lara Pau, Pedro Gil Corbacho, Amadeo Rey Cabieses, Antonio López de Ávila, Julio Carazo, Juan Carlos Campillo, Valentín Correal, José Luis López Jiménez, Antonio Vázquez Vega and Jaime Amuriza among others. I ask for forgiveness from anyone who might have been left out from this long list.

I would not want to end this long list of acknowledgements without mentioning my partner at this stage of my life, Eugenio de la Cruz Blázquez, who has always provided, and still does,

"unconditional support." I also thank my children Alex and Andrea, who as adults have encouraged me to strive for excellence. To all of you, with all my heart, thank you so much.

Alicia E. Kaufmann
Madrid, March 2008

The research for this book was sponsored by Centro de Investigaciones Sociológicas (CIS), which is financed by the Presidency, Madrid, Spain.

Foreword

This book could not come at a better time, just when the Spanish Parliament has passed legislation to achieve real equality between men and women. Commonly referred to as the Gender Equality Law, this document raises to the highest regulatory level the concept of "mainstreaming," which was coined at the 1995 World Conference on Women in Beijing as a tool to overcome the limitations of sectorial policies aimed at women. This initiative aims to bring an equality perspective to all of a state's policies and spheres of activity, from the economy to the environment, education, culture or the media. But the new Spanish law did not come out of the blue – rather, it rests on previous laws and a well-established social practice of parity in electoral rolls and in the makeup of state, regional and local ruling bodies. Even if not all political parties have embraced the decision to set specific quotas for women, those that did not – and who even criticized the concept – have been incorporating more and more women candidates into their lists with each election, which explains why the new law will be easy to implement. Gender equality is a concept that enjoys broad support in Spanish society, and there have been notable advances in the field in the last few years. However, there is one item that has sparked a heated debate and given rise to some criticism: the call for a balance between men and women on company boards within the next eight years. Boards still represent a hard core of economic power that women have barely been able to penetrate. And yet this is the final destination on the road towards upper management that Professor Kaufmann so accurately analyzes in this book.

As Professor of Sociology at the University of Alcalá de Henares, there is nobody better than her to tackle this complex task. Her broad research experience spans several countries and continents (Argentina, United States, France and Spain) as well as a variety of topics. She has touched upon social psychology and clinical cases concerning how to cope with serious diseases such as leprosy and cancer. Her expertise also extends to the sociology of organizations, with a special focus on the business world. No doubt this explains her

ability to understand the particular context in which female managers develop their careers as well as the specific set of dilemmas, doubts, expectations, desires and frustrations that these women experience.

Spain is an interesting case study because of the speed of sociological change – in other countries these changes have occurred over much longer periods of time. In little more than two decades, the working mother went from being an exception to being the rule in the new Spanish society. Until the 1960s, women could not be judges, yet today they make up the majority of that professional body. It was just 20 years ago that women were allowed to join the army and the security forces, but today they hold one out of every five jobs in those fields. A handful of women have also made it to the top of the business world – Amparo Moraleda, president of IBM Spain, and Ana Patricia Botín, president of Banco Español de Crédito, are good examples – but they are still few and far between.

Using discourse analysis techniques, this book uncovers a great many topics that underscore a new social change that is being spearheaded by women managers. It provides evidence of the tension between the old female obligation of selfless caregiving and helping others achieve their goals – the ethics of responsibility mentioned by Carol Gilligan, or the expressive leadership of Talcott Parsons – and the strong decision-making demands of an executive position. The book also explores the issues of ambition and money in the workplace, where the extreme circumspection evidenced by women managers is a good indicator of their sense of insecurity regarding these topics – whereas men display precisely the opposite attitude. Women in general, even those working their way to upper management, have trouble acting in their own best interest, a trait that was already described by John Stuart Mill as a difference between men and women, and one that the advocate of liberalism thought should be overcome. From a coherent liberal standpoint – which not all liberal thinkers have defended – the notion that what benefits an individual also benefits society must be extended to women, who share a common human nature with men. But as the results of this empirical research show, the female sense of responsibility towards others, rather than towards themselves, weighs heavily even today.

Female executives lack role models because the patterns inherited from their mothers do not apply to their present reality. But these patterns still show up in their self-doubt over personal identity, vocation

or even their behaviour as mothers if they have children of their own. Added to this is their insecurity over their own body image. Beauty is a widespread imperative that places huge demands on women and creates ambiguous situations regarding their professional status. There is a clear unresolved tension between the attributes expected of a woman and those expected of a leader. This strain is more extreme among the younger female executives, while older women display more relaxed attitudes. It is the combination of youth, power and the female gender that appears most difficult to accept.

The road traveled by women managers is often an uncertain and solitary one. They have little access to social support networks because men keep them out of their own, which are allegedly based on shared affinities created outside the workplace. But at the same time, women have not created their own mechanisms of gender solidarity. There are occasionally male mentors who play a key role in guiding and promoting women to positions of power within the company. Pygmalion emerges as an effective instrument on the hazardous journey across areas that used to be restricted to men.

It is especially interesting to compare the statements of the older interviewees – the first generation of women managers, who are now between 45 and 60 years old – and those of the younger 30-to-45 generation. The differences are noticeable and highly revealing. The older women embarked on their own careers with a certain degree of naiveté, believing that real and formal equality were one and the same, and that once basic obstacles like qualifications and personal ability were overcome, achieving their goals would simply be a matter of time and dedication. They also believed that the importance of motherhood and housekeeping had been overrated, and thought it perfectly possible to combine family and professional responsibilities. It is an attitude that clearly reflects the perspective of liberal feminism, or the *mystique of femininity* that was so well-defined by Betty Friedan. In this second period of their lives, these women are now suddenly aware of the hardships they've faced out of not wanting to give anything up – not the children, not the family, not the career. But at the same time they feel satisfied and proud of themselves for having managed to juggle everything.

The younger women seem much more cautious, more aware of the ground they are treading and more conscious of their own limitations. They plan more carefully for the future by weighing their

options: not having a partner, not having children, having them but postponing their ambitions, or having them only after reaching their career goals. But all of these choices entail some degree of renunciation that cannot but cause anxiety and frustration. The fact is – and these women know it well – it is still apparently not possible to have personal, emotional and professional development all at the same time. Their statements belie a certain bitterness: why is having a child not a problem for their male colleagues? We still know little about how men experience this process of change that women undergo – being workers and mothers at the same time – perhaps out of a common, if erroneous, belief that motherhood can go on affecting men only in a secondary way.

The last part of the book shows the results of the group discussions and interviews with managers who were asked about the growing female presence in top managing positions. These are topics that men have trouble talking about. This is partly due to their difficulties understanding and expressing emotions and generally anything to do with the private sphere; but it is also partly caused by a tendency to deny that women's issues are relevant or worthy of attention. Silence is a strategy of denial that some men still cling to.

The prevailing attitude that emerges from this research is a reluctance to accept the female presence in what is still perceived as a fundamentally male domain. This is particularly obvious when men have female bosses. A predominantly negative rhetoric is only tempered by statements associating women with maternal qualities such as promoting team work, cooperation and integration, or admitting that they are hard workers – perhaps an implicit reference to the female tendency to "make sacrifices for others." The most extreme case is represented by a manifest hostility towards women in positions of authority, including allegations of their inferior abilities. A variant of this ideological position reinterprets it in terms of "competitive differentiation," according to which women and men have complementary abilities whose potential is maximized in the private and public spheres, respectively. A third variant raises the ancestral fear of women by talking explicitly about the "danger" they represent when they attempt to cross barriers and control the work of men. There is some hope in the much more open and less defensive attitudes of younger men, who positively value female traits and women's way of exercising authority.

A joint analysis of the male and female perspectives sheds light on the scope of the challenge faced by women managers today. Their work environment is rife with difficulties that only a strong will and a commitment to develop one's abilities can overcome. Books such as this one help us understand an ongoing process of social change towards fairer and more equal relationships between men and women, and towards a society that makes the most of each of its members' potential.

Constanza Tobío
Professor of Sociology
Universidad Carlos III de Madrid

Author's Biography

Alicia E. Kaufmann is Professor of Sociology of Organizations at Universidad de Alcalá de Henares. She also holds a doctor's degree in Sociology from École des Hautes Études en Sciences Sociales in Paris and Universidad Complutense in Madrid. She is currently Academic Director at Alcalá de Henares and also teaches at Instituto de Empresa. She was a Fulbright scholar twice, once at Yale University and once at the University of Salzburg, where she specialized in leadership issues. Her teachers include Amando de Miguel, and Charles Perrow at Yale.

Her multicultural background (European parents, born in Argentina, Spanish children) opened up a range of interests and a curiosity for life that has led her to explore several different paths. In 1984 she was part of the executive team of the first Escuela de Gerencia Hospitalaria (Hospital Management School) in Madrid. Before that, between 1980 and 1983, she was on the first team to train Barcelona police officers on issues of social deviation and deviated conduct. From 1997 to 2000 she trained in London as a Tavistock Model consultant. She has also worked as a facilitator for Stephen Covey, author of *The Seven Habits of Highly Effective People*.

Her scientific work includes 18 books and 75 articles such as *Líder global: en la vida y en la empresa* (Global Leader in Life and at Work), published by Universidad de Alcalá de Henares in 1999, and *Construir equipos de trabajo en la era de la conexión* (Building Work Teams in the Connected Age), published by Universidad de Alcalá and Caja Madrid in 2003, with a foreword by Amparo Moraleda, president of IBM Spain). Her latest publication is about women's transition to upper management, Mujeres directivas: transición hacia la alta dirección published in *Opiniones y Actitudes*, No. 56, March 2007.

Kaufmann is an active member of FEDEPE, a federation of women in business. She was a creator, board member and director of the magazine Mujeres Directivas, and sits on the board of AECOP, a coaching association. She has two children who are "fortunately" no longer teenagers. Kaufmann is currently also teaching short courses on **Tools for effectiveness among female executives.**

E-mail address aliciak@wanadoo.es or alicia.kaufmann@uah.es

1

Introduction, Goals and Approach

Leaving aside the various studies and debates currently going on in Spanish society, the main goal of this research is to explore the causes that either hold back or foster women managers in their transition to higher level positions.

This work explores the elements that limit this process, such as those relating to social structure, family and professional socialization, education at its different levels, the possibility of reconciling work and family responsibilities depending on the woman's stage in the life cycle, and existing stereotypes within organizations regarding women in upper management.

As secondary goals, this study also wishes to explore the following issues:

1. Companies that move at hypervelocity create anxiety.
2. Attitudes toward hypervelocity: limits, renunciation or anxiety, depending on gender.
3. Exploring how the age factor conditions the social construction of identity.
4. Observing how ambition influences promotion possibilities.
5. Analyzing whether contacts and networks help access upper management positions.
6. Determining how higher education (MBA programs) opens doors to upper management.
7. Exploring role models (mother, father) and how this influences promotions.
8. Determining whether there is a differential socialization in terms of material goods.

9. Exploring the link between emotional intelligence and professional performance.
10. Examining whether motherhood is synonymous with employment discontinuity.

We believe that one of the reasons why no truly conclusive results have been obtained on some of these issues is the fact that most researchers looked no further than the external factors, both inside and outside the organization. We are of the opinion that, beyond those external factors, women managers are influenced by internal factors such as age and identity, which can prove crucial in order to understand the process of reaching and consolidating jobs in upper management.

Our initial premise is that people's expectations, whether men or women, change as they go through different periods in the life cycle (Kets de Vries[1]). That is why we will pay special attention to this variable, under the assumption that it is highly significant at the various stages of personal and professional development.

A second issue to take into account is the development of economic capacity resulting in financial independence. We live in a consumer society that equates ownership of material goods and money with power and authority; inversely, a lack of them creates low self-esteem. What we feel towards money will rule our lives. This is a topic on which people tend to be reserved, and this silence is even more marked among women.

Existing studies point out that the difference lies in the fact that women find it difficult to reconcile their roles as mothers and workers, and feel pulled between both jobs, while men for their part feel "trapped" by the need to make money, which ultimately becomes an expression of their manliness. This supposition is confirmed by CIS studies that show how men tend to attach greater value to financial security than women.

Our study showed that many adults remain faithful to the financial laws they learnt as children, which led us to try to disentangle the mental and emotional paradigms that block the road to financial freedom, and which often originated in childhood through the messages about money that we heard at home. These mental paradigms tend to color economic transactions with an emotional element.

For women, the social expectation of financial independence often clashes with the selfless attitude that is expected of her, making professional performance subordinate to caregiving, especially when it involves her immediate family. This conditioning factor varies depending on her stage of the life cycle. This research explores two different stages:

Adult life (30 to 45 years old): Existing studies (as well as testimony from interviews and group discussions carried out in this study) show that motherhood is overrated as the core of a woman's identity and that this condition is viewed by others as permanent.

Maturity (46 to 60 years old): This period can produce frustration due to the fact that the children are leaving home and to the difficulty of expanding personal horizons once the reproductive and educational roles are completed. This is the time for a woman to put her wishes ahead of other people's, to act on her own behalf rather than others', to move from selflessness to selfishness, to drop the "ball metaphor" – in other words, to stop making herself available to assist the play of others. We feel that the real innovation of our proposal lies in the incorporation and analysis of the interaction between the variables tied to formal education (basic and higher) and informal education (messages received from parents), as well as variables tied to emotional intelligence, the stage of the life cycle, and workplace socialization, including the issue of wages. All of these variables act as either facilitators or inhibitors of women's advancement from middle to upper management positions.

We will therefore explore the influence of family role models (father/mother), their capacity for stimulating or inhibiting personal ambition, and differences in attitude towards their male offspring (women's behavior and attitude towards her brothers, for instance). We will analyze how all of this affects women's self-esteem and either aids or blocks their access to upper management, while also helping create a new model for managing work relations that is often less harsh, and shows greater capacity for negotiation as well as conflict resolution.

At a second stage we will examine the influence of a woman's partner and his participation in the roles and tasks relating to family and reproduction. We will look at his capacity to happily accept her professional advancement, and to take on tasks that she has no time for. We believe that men have been socialized to be the main family

support, and if they do not achieve that position of provider many of them feel invalidated. For a woman's rise to upper management to stand a chance of success, it is crucial for her partner to accept a shift in roles and a redefinition of their identities.

A broad range of possible attitudes opens up here, from a partner's clear-cut opposition to acceptance and unconditional support. We believe that life as a couple brings into play the identities of both members, and that understanding organizational and personal readjustments requires a period of reflection about the emotional impact created by these changes.

Another topic that is explored in the interviews and group discussions is the impact of formal education, which does not always do enough to promote women's independence or to help them exercise control over their emotions, especially fear and guilt, two feelings that can prove paralyzing when social mandates are not fulfilled. Thus, a detailed analysis of the limitations created by each dimension (family, social and professional) will show us which aspects need to be reinforced in order to design specific seminars to fill the educational gaps that may be hindering women's access to positions of responsibility.

After exploring the personalities of women managers or women in a position to access upper management, we will examine their attitudes and conduct on the job at various stages of their career: as subordinates, as peers and as superiors, in their relationships with men and other women. First we will take a look at how they see themselves. We will also explore the male experience, and later analyze how they see women in relations of subordination, equality or seniority.

We must not lose sight of the fact that this is a purely qualitative study whose main strength lies in its heuristic nature and therefore its capacity to create hypotheses and suggest relationships that could only be empirically verified through a quantitative survey. Such a study has not yet been carried out, and it is quite obvious that it would be relevant to do so.

The results of this qualitative phase enabled us to design a questionnaire to determine in detail where the blockages occur. Its application to a representative sample of women in upper management positions on one hand, and to women with the potential to reach such positions on the other, would seem a highly recommendable endeavor.

The results of this second stage could lead to actions aimed at transforming these limiting factors into factors that underscore personal abilities and creating tools to help women fully develop their professional and emotional capacities.

2
Background

Existing literature

Interest in this topic is not recent; rather, it goes back to the 1980s, when it came to the attention of some researchers in the United States. But although there is abundant literature on gender and family violence, we cannot say the same about this issue.

The first studies were conducted by Rosabeth Moss Kanter[2] (1977), in her classic book *Men and Women of the Corporation*, a text that analyzes gender differences in higher positions. The originality of her formula lies in the fact that she takes an organizational approach to the role of occupational structure and all its labor-related factors. She came up with the famous line that power wears you out, but not having it wears you out even more. Following that line of thought, Kanter analyzed the segregated role of women inside the corporation, and how the fact that there are so few in upper management positions means that they effectively become the "tokens" who represent the rest of their social group. This is the reason why the women who make it to the top are viewed as representative symbols of the entire female community rather than as individuals. Belonging to such a minority group (only 4 percent in Spain) results in each one of their steps being carefully monitored and later extrapolated to the entire group. This is part of the reason why female managers experience loneliness in their position, a lot of pressure, isolation, a lack of other female references and exclusion from male networks. This nearly constant pressure erodes their self-assurance and self-esteem, and in some cases creates a strong feeling of guilt

because their potential mistakes could compromise the professional careers of other women. The same does not apply to men because, being in the majority, the entire group is not held responsible for individual mistakes made by one of its members.

According to Sarrió[3] there is also the "queen bee" phenomenon, consisting of women who have risen to the top on their own and have little sense of gender solidarity. They adopt male patterns that lead them to "not favor" the career of other women in order to avoid being accused of favoritism towards their peers, which would make them lose the respect of their male colleagues.

The last organizational model is the "showcase woman," a position created to make the company look more modern. The feelings produced by this type of job are very negative and in the long run, the position itself tends to be devaluated.

Later studies, hold that women face different hurdles according to the position they occupy in the organizational hierarchy, but that in general women have to deal with more obstacles than men. Other analyses indicate that women are usually excluded from informal networks and denied access to information that could help them improve their performance. Recent studies, in the United States, explored whether women have managed to break through the glass ceiling. These studies concluded that, even if the country has achieved equal pay at the highest levels, women managers faced another type of hurdle stemming from their difficulty in fitting into the prevailing male culture, which led to their treatment as a minority group.

In 1991, the American Association of University Women (AAUW), a federal organization devoted to the education of young women, conducted a survey on self-esteem among young men and women. The report, *Shortchanging Girls, Shortchanging America,* had significant media coverage and received widespread public attention. A nationwide survey was conducted to find out why after a 20-year struggle to achieve equal opportunities, many young women were unable to develop their full potential and achieve the things they had dreamed of. Some of the most significant findings were the following:

1. In primary school, 60 percent of girls and 67 percent of boys are "very happy with who they are." But in high school only

29 percent of girls are satisfied with themselves. The figure also dropped for boys, though significantly less: 46 percent still felt fully self-satisfied.

2. The explanation for this trend, according to the study, lies in the fact that young women realize that prevailing cultural values offer them fewer opportunities than boys to access non-traditional careers.

There used to be, and there still are, more male engineers than female engineers. These careers generally offer higher wages and greater opportunities. For men, self-esteem is mostly linked to "doing" while for women it is mostly linked to "being" and to relationships with others.

Parents and teachers play a major role in the construction or destruction of female self-esteem, in the sense that the prevailing culture holds that only success can generate more success. The more self-confident one is, the bigger the risks one is ready to take. There is often a strong correlation between self-esteem and careers in mathematics and other sciences. The study concluded that parents and teachers, and not peers, exert the greatest influence on the building of self-esteem and the formulation of high expectations in women (M. Bingham et al).[4]

A study edited by Mercedes Sánchez Apellániz[5] specifically analyzed this area and the evolution of women in upper management, a situation that the author holds is gradually improving. She points out that while in the United States female presence in upper positions is 30 percent, in Europe the figure drops to 20 percent and falls even more sharply when it comes to the very top posts, with remarkable differences between countries. Some of the factors that prevent women from reaching these positions is the lack of flexible working hours, the presence of biased communications and limits on access to training, all of which inhibits change within the corporate culture.

A more recent study by Infoempleo[6] based on in-depth interviews of 150 upper management workers in the public administration and the private sector shows that, contrary to the prevailing cliché about women's employment discontinuity, their careers in fact do have continuity. The study concludes that family concerns are less relevant than generally accepted, that traditional roles have been abandoned

as acceptable references, and that the hurdles to bigger promotions must be found in personal motives.

Another recent study by the Madrid regional government analyzed the paths to upper management positions and pointed to obstacles such as traditional family culture, the stereotype that holds that women have less availability than men for work, and the feeling that women have to prove themselves more than men. Family and partner support are crucial in overcoming these obstacles and moving up to top managerial jobs, but so are the possibilities of reconciling work and family life offered by the company.

Current international studies talk once more about "glass walls," indicating that women are being successful in selected industries often tied to new technologies.[7] There is also talk[8] about women being the best investment and representing the greatest potential for economic growth. Some applied psychology studies ask themselves whether men and women follow the same routes when climbing the corporate ladder.[9]

Some of the conclusions underscore that women consider their poor fit into the corporate culture, as well as their exclusion from informal networks, as hurdles to their rise up the organizational hierarchy. They minimize the importance of mentoring processes and indicate that they are given fewer opportunities for professional development in other countries. On this point, Iris Fischlmayr[10] analyzes the low female presence in international positions and the fact that most companies are unwilling to send women abroad, citing the problems they could encounter there by virtue of being a woman. Much has been written about the stereotypes and traditional roles of women, but a lot less has been said about how women themselves block their own access to upper management.

These earlier studies specifically tie in with our own object of research, besides the large amount of consulted material on the sociology of organizations, and theories on the return to the individual as proposed by Alain Touraine, Anthony Giddens and Charles Handy among others.

Film records

The deepest social changes have coincided in time with the development and expansion of film. The history of the 20th century is not

just a collection of stories from the past, but can be seen without the need for fictional reconstruction. Watching a few movies is enough to learn about people's preferences and lifestyles. By focusing on details that seem inconsequential, film brings us closer to the customs of another era and that, together with the characters' visual testimony, becomes an important tool in understanding recent history and understanding one another better. Despite all this, the use of film in the academic world is still very limited.[11]

One of the first films to represent "the gender earthquake" was *Thelma and Louise*. The main scene shows both women literally destroying the truck of a man who has been harassing them with obscene gestures and chauvinist comments.

In the 1996 screen adaptation of Olivia Goldsmith's novel *The First Wives Club*, three ex-wives of powerful businessmen get together after the death of a college friend to plot the best way to get back at the men for leaving them. One of them left his wife penniless, two other husbands cheated on theirs, and the fourth abused his. At first these women were very depressed and felt like victims, displaying self-destructive behavior. One began drinking, another started eating too much, yet another committed suicide and left a goodbye note explaining how her husband was hitting her. The remaining women created a club as a support group to deal with their indignation.

But this initial goal soon turned into a strategic plan based on the belief that things had to change. Their initial anger turned into the conviction that they had to attain power of their own. The women carefully analyzed their ex-husbands' weak points and built up an attack. In the process of taking over the men's companies, the women discovered their own strong points. They also became aware of their own difference when they said "If we only wanted revenge we would be just like them." But they want to be their own selves. That act of self-affirmation and the creation of the support group allows them to discover their own power and also their own wealth, understood as control over the material world.

The old myth about access to economic power through marriage is beginning to crack. The story of Cinderella and her romance with the prince as a way to escape poverty clashes with the story of Princess Diana, whose personality came to the fore after her divorce, to the point that she was able to challenge the entire British

monarchy. And these are just some examples of the type of reflection that we propose in this study, as would be some scenes from the movie *The Devil Wears Prada*, where Meryl Streep plays the powerful director of a fashion magazine with a very peculiar management style. The film shows how her character is able to manage her wealth and succeed in her line of work. She enjoys her job. This perception has been ratified by some of our interviewees, who said they enjoyed their work and saw it as a chance for personal and material growth.

3
Methodology

We opted for a qualitative methodology, considering it the best system – at least for this first exploratory phase – to explore the latent messages expressed by men and women on our subject of research.

The aim was not to compile standard statements by male and female managers (this would be the goal of a survey-based methodology), but to capture a freely flowing rhetoric, with no prior conditions and no pre-established categories.

The qualitative approach allows for an analysis of social reality from an emotional and individualized point of view, appropriate for a subject that requires a certain dose of introspection and self-analysis. Two different yet complementary qualitative techniques were used: in-depth interviews and group dynamics.

A total of 12 women and six men were interviewed, all of whom held upper management positions in their companies.

The 12 women managers devoted an average of two hours to the in-depth interviews. The group meetings all took place at the headquarters of the Fulbright Commission, whose director allowed us to use the rooms for this research. The positions held by these men and women ranged from general manager to communications chief, human resources director to independent consultant. Participating companies and organizations included Accenture, the Danish Embassy, Infoempleo, Gimnasio Metropolitan, Universia, Fundación Thyssen, Eurosport, Ferrovial, Asociación Fulbright, Banco Santander, Merck Sharp and Dohme, Adeslas, Mapfre, Banco Popular, British Petroleum, Delphi Metal, Agama Consultores, Caja Madrid, Robert

Allen-Horton, Global Estrategias, Fedepe, Aceme, Washington Quality Group, Brodeur Peon Worldwide and others. Our source for finding interviewees were the Instituto de Empresa Alumni Association, Aedipe (Association of Human Resources Managers), Dircom (Association of Communications Managers) and Fedepe (Spanish Association of Women Managers, Executives and Entrepreneurs).

This research would have been incomplete without including the male viewpoint. Six men were interviewed, all of them managers who worked independently or for other firms. Just as with the women, we tried to introduce a sufficient degree of demographic variety (age, marital status, children...) so as to cover all relevant situations.

The selection of interviewees were in the 30 to 60 age range. All marital situations were represented (married, single and separated). Some had children, some did not.

As for the group dynamics, three meetings were held in Madrid with an average attendance of six people per meeting. Their socio-demographic characteristics were as follows:

1. Female managers between 30 and 45 years of age.
2. Female managers between 46 and 60 years of age.
3. Male managers of both age groups.

The annex at the back of this book includes the outlines used in the in-depth interviews and the group discussions.

Choosing a qualitative methodology does not close the door to the possibility of exploring our topic from different perspectives. The material that we collected and analyzed resulted in a draft questionnaire that we feel would, if applied to a survey, be a helpful guide to reach a deeper understanding of the obstacles that women encounter on their way to "the top."

This questionnaire (a potential survey to be conducted after the first exploratory phase) is the best way to broach such a complex issue. The interviews and group dynamics gave us a glimpse into the main issues that these women (and men) feel are important, without adding preconceived notions on our part. To gauge and quantify the importance of each of these issues is something that should be done later, and is doubtlessly just as important. It will allow us to verify the relevance of our preliminary hypothesis through quantitative analysis.

Preliminary hypotheses

- The greater the speed and pressure, the harder it becomes to reflect on one's own life and priorities.
- Women show a greater need for integration (work and family) and a greater tendency to experience frustration and renounce certain rights.
- Women tend to be less ambitious, and have fewer networks of contacts as well as less training (MBA), all of which holds them back from upper management jobs.
- Women have fewer role models at work, leading to an uneven career development.
- The older the woman, the more consolidated her identity, while the younger women are more confused by the pressure and hypervelocity of society.
- Women have greater difficulties managing material goods and a lower self-esteem that prevents them from demanding equal pay.
- Emotional belief that the greater the professional or financial success, the worse one's personal life will be (divorce). This can be a career obstacle.
- The greater the tension (fears and insecurity), the worse material issues will be managed.
- While men seem more attracted to risk, women display a greater aversion to it.
- Women are educated in dependency (fear), not in self-sufficiency.
- Women are no less ambitious than men, but they simply have to reduce their expectations in order to reconcile their duties.

4
Characteristics of 21st Century Organizations

Analysis of the technological environment

In order to understand why female attributes contribute greatly to 21st century organizations, we will review the characteristics of global corporations and how they condition personal relationships. Our starting point will be the influence of the technological environment.

According to Jeremy Rifkin,[12] we are organizing life at the speed of light. Each day sees the introduction of new computer programs and new information technologies that compress time, accelerate activity and process increasing volumes of information in the shortest time. At first this technology offered the hope of a more comfortable life by liberating us from certain tasks and providing us with more free time. But nowadays, after investing huge amounts of money in such technologies, we need to ask ourselves whether they really make us free or rather ensnare us in a network of ever-faster connections. A new term, "24/7," makes reference to our new time frontiers. There is 24-hour availability through e-mail, voice mail, automatic teller machines, services that try to capture our attention at any time of the day or night...We are starting to feel that we have less time now than at any other moment in recent history.

All of this points to our being immersed in a world where time is much more complex and interdependent than ever before, a world made up of networks of changing relationships and activities. A world where each available minute becomes an opportunity to make a new connection. Descartes' famous phrase "I think, therefore I am" has

been replaced by "I am connected, therefore I am." What happens when our lives are immersed in relationships 24 hours a day and these move at the speed of light?

We observed internal and external clues to the unease felt by people over this lack of time. There is alarming epidemiologic data about the increase of stress-related diseases. According to experts, many of these illnesses are due to people's incapacity to permanently keep up the current pace and intensity of human activity, which moves at almost the speed of light. In the United States, over 43 percent of the active population suffers from the adverse effects of stress. This costs millions of dollars for companies that have to deal with absenteeism, lower productivity, worker rotation and medical expenses. Illnesses such as depression, heart and brain strokes, high blood pressure, heart attacks, cancer and diabetes are growing at alarming rates among young and middle-aged people, and could become the main causes of sick leave in our information age.

The excessive speed of our new 24/7 society has other profound consequences on people's lives. Round-the-clock commercial and social activity has led to a sharp decline in our hours of sleep. In 1910 the average adult slept between 9 and 10 hours a day. Nowadays, adults in highly industrialized societies sleep an average of 5 to 7 hours a day. This means we are awake an extra 500 hours a year. This massive lack of sleep created by our frantic pace is also linked with the medical problems described earlier.

The age of speed brings with it a lack of reflexiveness and a certain amount of confusion regarding the ethical values that guide people's conduct. It is possible to observe a marked lack of social responsibility that a few socially responsible companies are trying to do something about. Perhaps we should ask ourselves what type of connections really matter in the age of economics and electronics, and what the impact of this hypervelocity is on people's quality of life.

Analysis of the organizational environment

This part of the study explores the characteristics of the new corporation in our technology-driven, globalized society and its effects on people. The new economy requires flexible firms that can quickly respond to the tensions created by the new technologies and global markets. This so-called "flexibility" includes flexible working hours

Table 4.1   Characteristics of the Technological and Organizational
Environment

Technological determinants	Effects on people
• New 24/7 frontiers • Lighting speed relationships • Lack of time and sleep • Stress-related diseases • Speed equals lack of reflexiveness • Morals of relativity • Scant emotional connections • Possibility of working from home • Unlimited access to knowledge • Predominance of networks	• Technological dependence • Low commitment to work • Depersonalized relationships • Employment discontinuity • Little differentiation between work and personal matters • Unlimited schedules • Culture of risk versus fear of failure • Difficulty building a workplace identity

and flexible contracts (or part-time ones), the outsourcing of production and job instability.

The new forms of production require individuals who can adapt
quickly to changing companies and environments, the social consequences of which can alter a worker's social and job situation over a
short period of time. Amid a diversity of changes, there are a few
which are especially significant:

1. **Low commitment to the job**: the speed of change, the lack of
   information, a sense of uncertainty and a lack of trust makes
   people feel less committed to the task they have been assigned.
2. **Technological dependence**: if for some reason technology fails
   at a given moment, the worker may feel useless and incapable of
   creatively resolving the situation.
3. **Difficulty building a workplace identity**: Constant rotation
   and the diversity of positions held by each worker hinders the
   development of a progressive work experience that could forge a
   workplace identity. Additional problems are short-term projects
   and the constant risk of unemployment or early retirement.
4. **Employment discontinuity**: Nothing is long-term (there are
   few professional careers within a given company). There is low
   commitment and loyalty to the firm. Loyalty is felt for one's
   career, but not for the organization. Solid links only emerge
   in long-term relationships, and they also depend on the others'

predisposition to make commitments. In the case of women, this interruption is significantly conditioned by their biological clock, and is more clearly observable around the age of 30.

5. **Social and family dislocation**: This job system does not favor identification with other members of the organization due to the constant rotation and lack of participation. The favored behavior is based on one of Bion's basic assumption groups: the dependency group. It is possible to observe permanent attempts at reconciling work and family even when the demands of the job are excessive and interfere with these attempts.

6. **Little differentiation between the personal and work spheres**: With new technologies, there is no real separation between the various spheres of life (one works longer at home or else spends many hours at work). According to Richard Sennett, we are facing the problem of how to organize our personal life in a capitalist system that disposes of people and at the same time sets them adrift.

7. **Depersonalized relationships**: The 21st century corporation has led to a loss of stable links and of the sense of belonging to a group. Until the 1980s, the company was a social system "against anxiety" but these days corporations have become "creators of anxiety."

8. **A culture of risk versus fear of failure**: Market conditions force people to take on risks even if the rewards are meagre. The instability inherent to flexible organizations exposes people to repeated burnout. Accumulated experience is not highly valued, and workers live in a climate of ambiguity and uncertainty.

Until now we have analyzed the features of global society as well as of organizations and their effects on people. In Spanish society, a CIS study compared 1987 and 2002 values, and found a decline in the importance given to work.

A closer analysis reveals that these divergences in the attitude towards work in various European societies stems from their GDP. In order to reach the same level of welfare as other countries, Spaniards are forced to invest more hours to achieve the same results. Specific job-related results of the study showed that Spaniards felt "almost twice as much pressure" in 2002 as they did in 1987. This leads us to conclude that, on top of the trans-

Table 4.2   The Company Both Contains and Creates Anxiety

Company	
Contains anxiety	Creates anxiety
• Promotes stability	• Social and family dislocation
• Allows for work and leisure time	• No time limits
• Allows for projective systems	• Inhibits projective systems and
• Social cooperation redistributes	the construction of a workplace
negative impulses	identity
• Job continuity facilitates	• Predominance of basic
creation of a social identity	assumption behavior

Source: Produced by author

formations brought on by globalization, the pressure exerted on individuals is sufficiently intense as to warrant the need for some kind of support at the workplace.

The previous table attempts to explain how, up until the 1990s, companies were development centers for people. A relative job stability, regular schedules and dealings with other colleagues favored healthy, stable relationships within the firm.[13] With the globalization of society, things changed radically. Mergers and acquisitions, company outsourcing, the fall of the Berlin Wall, the Internet era, the massive arrival of workers from less-developed countries and the competition from China and India are some of the factors that have radically changed the situation, in such a way that companies that used to provide support for workers now, do the exact opposite. Neverending work hours, expatriations and virtual links condition the individual to live "in a state of permanent tension" (basic assumption state). This has a negative impact on all levels of life for people and corporations, who find it hard to satisfy their basic human needs.[14]

5
Identity Dimensions: Women Managers and Motherhood

Identity dimensions

We believe that due to the social pressure exerted by modern corporations, it becomes necessary to examine how the workplace identity is constructed in a global society.

> We define identity as the capacity to keep feeling like oneself amid the succession of transformations that are the basis of a person's emotional experience. This involves maintaining stability throughout the various changes that occur in life.

Personal evolution involves an uninterrupted series of transitions. Understanding them helps build a sense of identity. Lack of understanding, on the other hand, leads to stagnation and to the repetition of old behavioral patterns that hinder the rise to the upper echelons of a company.

In our globalized and technology-driven society, there are many question marks regarding the definition of this concept. What is the nature of what we call identity? It is a structure, a symbol, something that is bestowed on us by the position we hold at work; it is a link, a strong bond that keeps the person together. It is a relationship in a multiplicity of relationships and networks. It is a feeling, or the expression of an unconscious fantasy. It is how we see ourselves, or how others see us. Is it there since the beginning of life, or

is it gradually consolidated in the course of evolution? All these questions have to do with identity.

But this changes radically in a globalized society. The terms identity, identification, equality, differentiation are not interchangeable, but rather point to specific aspects of a person that need to be distinguished. Zygmunt Bauman[15] points to the changes that have taken place in contemporary times regarding the notion of identity. He says that nowadays, people's lives elapse in a liquid element where the concept of identity has become ambiguous. He says identity is a concept that divides even when it wants to unite and excludes when it wants to divide. We observed this slipperiness described by Bauman in our interviews with women managers. Their attitudes ranged from prioritizing to giving up certain things, as we can gather from the following statements:

> I have never wanted to get any further because I need to have a personal life. There was a moment here when I might have made the jump to upper management, but I didn't want to. I feel content professionally, and I have time for other things. We women know how to set the limits... (Manager, 53 years old)

> Right now I could possibly be working at a consulting firm or an engineering company, but I would be at the same level. When you want something and you do what it takes, you get what you want in the end. (Manager, 55 years old)

> I believe in willpower. I don't look back and say "oh, I was so lucky." It seems to me that everything I have I achieved through work and effort. By giving, rather than receiving. (Manager, 49 years old)

There is a very feminine comment here, "giving, rather than receiving," not believing in good luck but in personal effort and perseverance. Another element is knowing how to set the limits, first with oneself and then with others. This means accepting a certain amount of frustration, which is a sign of emotional maturity.

This notion of limit and renunciation appears much more frequently in statements by women than in statements by men, as does a certain amount of flexibility to accept this reality.

They asked me to join the team in France and to head the communications department for all of Europe. My little girl was 2 months old and my family is in Madrid, so I didn't think it was a very good idea. But I did it for two years, managing a 12 million-euro budget, and that was a key moment for me. Today I manage southern Europe, Greece, Malta, Turkey, Israel, Portugal, all of that. That's what I do. (Manager, 33 years old)

Research by Sennett[16] points out that modern capitalism does not merely extract people's added value, but their identities as well. The company is no longer a place for integration, a protective group that creates new reference points. Other work by Piñuel[17] describes "mobbing" experiences at work, as well as "toxic bosses" and their victims,[18] which also affects the identities of individuals.

A woman is capable of sizing up her possibilities and negotiating first with herself and later with the company, giving things up in alternative ways according to her priorities at each stage of her life cycle.

At first I turned it down. I didn't have much of a choice, I said something like: "My child is 2 months old, but I'll handle it until we find the right person." (Manager, 33 years old)

The effects of hypervelocity on identity (J. Rifkin)[19] include having trouble finding a space to think and to emotionally digest events that occur at lightning speed. This statement needs to be explained through the personal life experiences of the interviewees.

I'm the type of person who does not like limitations, I am terribly bored by routine. People ask me "When do you rest?" I do that when I read something about my profession. I am stuck because I enjoy what I do and in the end it becomes a trap. For instance I was unable to do the one thing I do just for my own sake, which is go to the gym. Instead I had a work lunch. (Manager, 46 years old)

Right now, changes in the workplace and in society are undermining the health of managers who had placed their trust in the company and in the stability of social relations.

I feel that time is passing and that I am lost. I lost moments with my children, although I didn't realize it at the time. Sometimes we get in a reflexive mood and I ask them if they would have liked a different type of mother. They ask me for more time, but if I hadn't done what I like to do, I would have brought home feelings of frustration and edgy nerves. (Manager, 45 years old)

The interviewees showed signs of the effects of hypervelocity, the idea of wanting to do everything, the omnipotence (perfectionism) of not seeing the limits and their costs. According to François Dupuy,[20] one could see the organizational changes that would upset work conditions and explain the current unease felt by many managers, as seen in the previous statements.

These upper managers make up the pool of "trustworthy paid personnel" whose positions are being subjected to a process of increasing vulnerability. Following this author's line of thought, upper managers come out of this process in better shape than other groups because of their training. Regarding their global position within the company, the treatment they get, how they are evaluated, promoted, replaced and so on, their situation is becoming increasingly similar to that of other employees.

But two items hit upper managers harder than other workers. First, the traditional individualism of executives, their talent, their singularity, in short, "the aggregate personal value."

Secondly, vulnerability hits them hard because they are ill-equipped to present collective responses to a given problem. Instead they display a massive individual vulnerability. The trait that defined them now turns against them. As a result of globalization there is an inverse situation. Before, clients and shareholders were relegated to a secondary position, but in the last few years this dynamic has changed and executives are the first victims of change. Their earlier autonomy is being replaced by a constant evaluation of their performance.

When identity flows without any major setbacks, it appears not to exist. But in our days, given the speed of change, identity has become a chief preoccupation and one needs to be constantly asking oneself who she or he is. This self-questioning is part of the process of getting to know and recognize one's own identity. As

Table 5.1   Dimensions of Identity

1. **Personal**: the parts that make up the self
2. **Temporal**: oneself at different moments in life
3. **Social**: being part of social networks and using mechanisms of identification and projection
4. **Geographical**: place of birth and effects of expatriation
5. **Work-related**: effects of the environment and the organization on the individual
6. **Gender-related**: differences between sex (biological aspects) and gender (cultural perception)

a first approximation, we can distinguish between five levels of identity:

The key lies in continuing "to feel like oneself" despite the changes, and in synthesizing the transitions in order to develop one's potential. An emotionally mature identity is one that can accept the frustration and loss inherent to life and rebuild learnt models. To manage this, one must go through periods of confusion and psychological disorganization, break with consolidated aspects of one's personality and facilitate the construction of a new identity.

When it comes to workplace identity, it is possible to distinguish between several aspects of the same. At work, we can observe a change from "loyalty and protection" towards a different hegemonic model based on "competition and evaluation." Executives' commitment to their firm is limited in time, because they have noticed that the bonds that tie them to the firm are no longer what they used to be. In large organizations, "soft socialization" no longer exists. Whoever joins an organization is immediately immersed in a world that leads to a great state of confusion in the face of so much vulnerability. This feeling is exacerbated by the transition of women to positions traditionally held by men.

Differences in identity by gender

There is a significant difference in identity when it comes to men and women. According to the testimony gathered in this study, women are historically conditioned by their biological identity: menstruation, motherhood and menopause. A man's identity is mainly built around the work dimension. His transition to upper

management positions lacks biological interruptions, allowing for a linear and continuous career evolution. Confusions arise in the statements about sex (biological level) and gender (cultural component), which in turn leads to a certain incapacity to understand the differences between both.

This general idea is supported by the personal experiences of the interviewees:

> I got married and had two children...I never stopped working, although you don't have the same energy when you get a call telling you that your two year-old has the measles and is running a 40-degree fever and you need to run home. You're not there 100 percent. Five years after having one child I had another one. But that's a mistake, you should have children one right after the other to get it over with. (Manager, 53 years old)

According to Carol Gilligan[21] the main question lies in knowing how we relate to others, given that our lives are profoundly linked at the psychological, economic and political levels. Gilligan points to gender differences: whereas a man defines his identity through separation (from his mother), a woman defines hers through bonding.

> I travel a lot and I am missing out on part of my little girl's life. You can't do everything 100 percent. I need the salary I make. I spend as much time as I can with my daughter, but maybe I am losing out a bit in that area. I didn't go work in Paris because of my family, to be able to see my grandparents while they're still around, I don't know how long that will be. You always give something up. (Manager, 33 years old)

A woman's difficulty to carry out a fundamental separation, not only from her mother but also from other members of her family such as children or, as in the former case, grandparents, can be an important limiting factor.

Sigmund Freud wrote that women's identity is a bit blurred and that while men perceive reality "through logic and the law," women perceive life through communication and relationships. He also said that women are more conditioned by "an ethics of nurturing" whereas for men, the prevailing ethic is one of power.

Men and women perceive danger differently. While men are wary of connections born out of intimacy, women see a greater danger in success, born out of a competitiveness that can result in loneliness, feelings of desolation and a sense of not being loved. In short, this means that men and women experience "attachment" and "separation" in different ways, and each one perceives "dangerous" personality aspects that the other does not perceive at all.

I started working on a project covering all of Spain, traveling every week. You learn about different ways of doing things, but it kind of ruins your personal life. You start getting more and more detached from your group of friends, your family. You don't see them every day anymore. (Male manager, 37 years old)

We observe that continuous separations are experienced differently. Whereas for men it is more customary, for women the effects of expatriation take the shape of concern.

Competitiveness and aggression are experienced by women as a threat to their desire to make a connection. That is why autonomy can be viewed as a risky situation, which might explain why women are more dependent on other people's approval. The transition to motherhood is a great change because women go from a situation of selfishness to one of being responsible for another human being. But caring for others first means caring for oneself. Carrying out this task represents the transition towards emotional maturity.

People have children when they're studying, so their own mothers can take care of them. If you start having them when you're working, you can't. Before we used to have children when we were very young. I had my little girl when I was 22, so when I was 30 she was already eight years old. When you have a two year-old and a month-old baby, that's an impossible situation. (Manager, 49 years old)

On the other hand, this crucial experience for the survival of the species is handled alone and with little help from society. According to Naomi Wolf[22] each year millions of women's lives are turned around by the decision to have a child. This places them in a paradoxical situation: on one hand they are about to undergo one of the

most fascinating experiences in the life of a woman, but at the same time it is a solitary, sensual and highly debilitating experience, both physically and mentally. A new being will initially depend entirely and totally on its mother. On the other hand, society trivializes this reality and sends out culturally childish messages that do not acknowledge the enormous effort it takes to be a mother and a working professional at the same time.

> We want it all and I think that women are getting this reconciling business mixed up. It is possible to work and care for your family at the same time, but you cannot be the best at work and still have the same kind of time for your family. One is incompatible with the other. When my children were all grown up I asked myself "Did I neglect them?" and I asked my daughter: "Bea, did you miss your mother's presence?" and she said "No, because you were there when I needed you." (Manager, 53 years old)

On the other hand, a man who does not embrace paternity loses sensitivity and the chance for emotional growth that this process offers. At the organizational level, he barely develops other people's potential. And we must not forget gender socialization. Integration and reconciliation could take place with greater ease if we educated people in "the colors of the rainbow" instead of in pink and blue.

> Education does a lot. You grow up in an environment where it's the father who brings home the money and you are taught that you must marry and take on your husband's status. That used to be the lesson. (Manager, 53 years old)

It is possible to observe a different emphasis on material things, which we will analyze in greater detail in Chapter 8. As far as attitudes towards everyday life are concerned, traditional stereotypes make men more afraid of loneliness and women more afraid of being left. Often, apparently innocuous patterns hide factors that place limits on women's capacity for thought, action and decision-making. In terms of negotiation we see that while men either negotiate or enforce their will, women yield to appease others and avoid their getting angry. This means that they are the ones to contain their own anger, which later turns into depression. Often a link will

Table 5.2   Differences in Identity According to Gender

	Men	Women
Fears	Failure	Rejection
Needs	Separation	Bonding
Focus	On oneself/selfishness, narcissism	On others/altruism, ball metaphor
Family socialization	Single role. Ethics of power	Several roles. Ethics of nurturing
Career evolution	Continuous	Discontinuous
Organizational behavior	More action and decision-making	More emotion
Career priorities	Salary/competitiveness/ reaching the top	Diversion, integration, good work environment

Source: Produced by author

emerge between independence and loneliness, which is why some women tend to make themselves indispensable. There are many gender-related mental traps and blind spots, and this is one of them.

Identity and the crossroads of motherhood

Without a doubt, the biggest differentiating trait between men and women is fertility. This became manifest throughout the study, independently of the age range being analyzed. Most female participants brought up the subject of motherhood spontaneously in the group meetings. Having children, as a vital and total event[23] in the life of a woman, conditions her as a person and as a professional. The economics journalist Ann Crittenden, in her book *The Price of Motherhood*, explains that two thirds of all wealth is created by human ability, creativity and an entrepreneurial spirit, known as "human capital." This means that parents who raise their children consciously and effectively are the biggest creators of wealth in our economy. The education system also contributes to the creation of human capital by guiding people's productivity in order to make

them more effective at work. But children who do not grow up under stable and attentive caregivers in safe homes do not get as much out of this education system.

This job transformation not only results in a greater dedication to childrearing to the detriment of working hours, but it also develops qualities that can add to a woman's managing skills by promoting employees' potential.

One aspect of motherhood that needs to be taken into account is the degree to which it takes away from her dedication to her professional career, especially in highly demanding areas such as upper management.

Interviewees showed a clear difference according to gender. Many of the men believed that the issue of motherhood was strictly a woman's business and should therefore be resolved by her. These comments showed a great confusion, given that whereas a person's sex is determined by biological aspects relating to reproduction, gender is specific to the human race and has complex attributes determined by culture. The confusion of these visions is reflected in some of the comments made by both male and female managers.

> I wonder who is going to show more dedication to the job, who will not stop coming in to work when the kid needs to be taken to the doctor. We hire without discriminating here, but as a manager I tell myself: I have these two [candidates] who are similar, but next year this woman will get married and have a child, and if she has a child what will happen? This guy will leave if he doesn't get a promotion, and vice versa... (Male manager, 48 years old)

This type of comment shows the confusion, lack of understanding and influence of gender stereotypes, by which we mean the system of beliefs about the supposed traits shared by a group. This social construction does not always coincide with reality, given that motherhood is not a permanent state, but instead requires a profound commitment for a limited period of time. On the other hand, it is not a woman's problem but a project shared by the couple.

> I think women make a choice. They say "I am giving up this competition, because I have other priorities." Our biggest rota-

tion is in consulting, we keep them for six or seven years, they are highly trained, and that coincides with the ages of 30 or 31, when people usually get married, have kids and opt for a more comfortable life. (Male manager, 46 years old)

We notice here the double vision, that of the employer who is thinking about what is more immediately profitable in economic terms, and the attempt at showing empathy with the woman by assuming that she is choosing motherhood because it is more comfortable, which means the company no longer feels the obligation to support one of its managers for a limited period of time.

> I think that women, when they have to make a choice, choose family life. They would rather consolidate than reconcile. Tell the Chinese or the Indians about reconciling work and family. It's a matter of choice. I admit it's harder for women. (Male manager, 45 years old)

As the in-depth interviews and group meetings progressed, it became more obvious that from the male point of view the female identity is mainly marked by her biology, with her identity and career development a far-off second. At no time does it appear that the company has a social responsibility – rather, it is a personal situation that the woman has to resolve on her own.

> I had the opportunity to participate in seminars about reconciling work and family. For a woman this is harder. For a man it is more common to sacrifice his personal life. There is no need to rend our vestments over it. It is simply that women are biologically designed to have children. (Male manager, 42 years old)

Regardless of age or sector in which they work, men's vision appears to be short-term, given that a person's performance and experience yield results in the mid-to-long-term. Their observations are the product of a patriarchal culture with a series of norms, values and prejudices that predetermine a woman's need for giving something up, without any involvement on their part. Whereas women's statements almost always show concern for the other, the man's

attitude is adverse to the development of women's careers within the corporation.

I am a well-organized person, very orderly. We are immersed in a culture of presence, not productivity...I have on occasion left meetings because I had to go to the daycare center. I have held positions of responsibility in human resources, at a multinational firm. After a maternity leave I was told not to bother coming back, and this sort of thing is not as infrequent as you'd think... (Manager, 43 years old)

A man who was asked if he would have made the same decisions had he been a woman, said:

If I had been a woman I wouldn't have had kids. It's really important to work in order to develop mentally, otherwise you turn into a parasite. If I had decided to be a mother, I would have married a really rich guy or else chosen a job that didn't take up a lot of my time so I could care for them. (Male manager, 42 years old)

We observed great gender differences in opinions about motherhood. For men it is a "woman's problem" and a motive for career discontinuity, whereas for women it is not a traumatic event, on the contrary. There is also a difficulty in distinguishing between the social side of maternity as a basic element for the survival of the species and the business side of it, consisting of providing assistance to carry out the reproductive process. Women, and mothers especially, manage people differently; instead of controlling they try to liberate people's potential, which is the management style most needed in the 21st century in order to retain talented employees.

I hired a man not long ago and he went and took a paternity leave because his wife is self-employed and couldn't. I think that's fine, it's his right to do so, but this man is gone from the project and I can't get him back on board later. (Male manager, 42 years old)

Given the unavoidability of the subject for both men and women, both genders should reflect together in order to overcome the obsta-

cles of an issue that affects everyone. But there is little solidarity towards motherhood. In this sense, reconciliation policies should be supported at all levels – businesses, government and society – and extended to all, as single people without families are also entitled to reconciling work and personal life.

> We women have to reconcile. Fortunately my husband has supported me throughout my career. I think that behind every great woman there is also a great man. For instance, I had cancer and needed treatment and I couldn't get pregnant, so we decided to adopt a child. We started doing all the paperwork, and a month later I got pregnant. When my child was one year old a project came up concerning a firm with 350 female employees that might shut down and leave them all jobless. It meant going to Texas for three months, with a one year-old...Then my husband said: "If you don't take the job because you think I wouldn't be a good father, I'd be disappointed." So I took on the project. (Manager, 55 years old)

> My life was very well organized when my partner wasn't here – we couldn't talk until the weekend. Suddenly, having him around every day at home makes me feel like I'm not taking care of the children anymore. Now I have the time to get up in the morning, have breakfast, get dressed, and even take a shower without bringing all three of them into the tub with me. I remember friends telling me they wouldn't like their children to see them naked. But what could I do? I couldn't leave them running around the house while I showered, because anything could happen. Now it's as though I'd gotten married again. (Manager, 36 years old)

We see that when both members share responsibilities, as in the previous two cases, reconciling work and family is possible, but there must be a commitment on both sides. The family models that people were raised with, are also important.

> My mother was a mathematics and physics teacher, and in the end we girls all studied one or the other, so she had quite an influence over us. She was a woman who always said that the important thing is not how much time you spend on your

children, but that it be quality time. They put in our heads the notion of not wasting time. So now we are unable to relax. (Manager, 55 years old)

Nowadays, younger generations are starting to perceive changes in their fathers' commitment and emotional development. They are becoming aware of the passage of time and of the benefits of a father figure, especially for the psychological development of the child's identity.

Young men have realized that it's worth it to be a father. A 50 year-old man does not want to come home and find his wife asking him to bathe the children or help them with their homework. Now men eat in 45 minutes and try to be home early. I am convinced that there is going to be a domino effect. Young people are not prepared to stay at work beyond 7pm. Young parents want to be with their children. A great cultural change is under way. (Manager, 41 years old)

Now that this nuance between family and personal reconciliation has been sketched out, we will develop two more issues: the dedramatization of motherhood, which in reality is the way in which women often perceive this part of their lives; and the development of positive managing skills acquired by managing the family unit that, once applied to the workplace, increase professional effectiveness.

Taking the drama out of motherhood

To do this, we must first realize that women, like men, are not one-dimensional beings. They can and must play several roles during their lives, setting priorities and assigning values to the different roles at various stages of their life cycle. Motherhood is not forever, as the need for greater commitment usually occurs in the first few years. This interruption is sanctioned by leaving the woman out of the loop, especially from the male point of view, as we can see from the references made in the following comments:

I had a daughter at 25 and…well, there were not many people of my generation who were working then. Here in Spain we studied,

many of us went to college, some worked, but if you got married that was it...there were not many married women working at the time. (Manager, 53 years old)

During Spain's transition to democracy, it was normal for women to work only for exceptional reasons, a situation that is completely inverted nowadays. That is why, in some cases, it is necessary to break with the inherited role of the traditional mother. The female manager is not exclusively devoted to her children, but neither are other women who do not hold upper management positions. That is why it is important to relieve that sense of guilt towards one's own children, and also towards the company, as we can see in the following interview:

I was at a selection process with some clients. She was the one who said: "What will you do if the kids get sick?" I told her: "Right now I could smash you against the wall." But you find a lot of people like that. Now I work on my own. (Manager, 44 years old)

Women's situation these days can be one of multidimensional guilt, as well as overblown omnipotence, in that she may believe that she alone has to take care of everything without any assistance from her partner. Otherwise she would feel bad. When she finds herself face to face with her partner, she feels guilty for not playing the traditional role that she is supposed to play within the family. She feels guilty towards the company because her presence could be requested at any moment, and while at an important meeting she could get a call from school telling her that her child is ill. And she feels guilty towards her children, who demand her attention. But there are also cases where instead of feeling guilty, women set limits and priorities when it comes to managing their time.

I certainly don't feel guilty because I love my job, I think it's really interesting. I've sometimes been told that I never had to learn how to say no because I get carried away by my own enthusiasm, and I have to be really tired before I'll say no. (Manager, 34 years old)

I think that in some cases we place really high demands on ourselves. I am very organized, I've been told that I seem German because I plan my year, my periodical meetings, although later I sometimes have to move things around in my agenda because you also need to be flexible. But sometimes I think we fall into this pattern of goals that...personally, I have gone so far as to establish not only my career goals but also my personal goals. (Manager, 36 years old)

I am going to learn how to say no. Last Thursday I left work at six, and I had a headache. The cocktail party was at eight. I asked myself if I felt like going, and I didn't. So I took the car and went home, which is what my body wanted me to do. Had it been an unavoidable obligation...but sometimes there are things you can say no to. You have to learn to take care of yourself a bit. (Manager, 35 years old)

Women, more than men, tend to set limits on themselves and others, both in their personal and professional lives. This is very helpful when it comes to not forcing the body and mind beyond reasonable levels. Sometimes, women's demands on themselves lead to levels of exhaustion that go beyond the manageable, and occasionally result in anxiety attacks. Today we can observe the "tired woman's syndrome."

Often women, just because they happen to be female, have to care for others – parents, siblings. When it comes to motherhood, women can bring an added value to people management. Motherhood develops emotional abilities that benefit relationships between people in an organization and help manage teamwork.

1. Capacity for encouraging teamwork
One of the maternal qualities is to encourage a child's development in terms of intellectual capacity and personal skills.

2. Capacity for encouraging emotional bonds
Large multinational corporations are seeing their leader figures grow weaker as increasingly rigid and anonymous structures are put in place. Achieving an emotional link with the employee is a synonym

of motivation and identification that is very positive for the work environment and for getting results.

3. *Capacity to absorb tension without projecting it on the rest of the group*
Analogous to the role played within the family.

4. *Capacity for developing a more defined workplace identity*
In the hypervelocity age it is very difficult to develop a personality.

5. *Capacity for integrating team differences*
Globalization affects all levels of society and the composition of teams carrying out diverse tasks. In this sense, the skills developed while caring for children offer an interesting chance to integrate the different identities that make up large corporations.

6. *Adaptation to change, speedier processes*
Modern organizations require adaptation to change in the most efficient and speedy manner possible. A logic based on static, distant and severe leaders does not offer the best tools for dealing with new challenges. That is why managing human resources from a point of view that takes into account specific needs is a good bet.

7. *Capacity for time management*
Another one of the skills developed by women is making the most of time, or living in stereo as some interviewees put it. This capacity for multitasking is an excellent way to develop a new form of work that is not based on 12 hours of physical presence at work, but rather on good time management.

8. *Capacity for setting priorities*
Another distinctive female trait is the notion of limits, probably because of women's greater bond with time and the lifegiving cycle. We must not forget that a woman's inner calendar marks the passage of time. The onset of fertility-menstruation when a girl becomes a woman marks the passage of the months. Then there are the nine months before a child is born, the arrival of menopause and maturity, and so on. These are events that teach us about the passage of time, and with it the notion of limits in our lives. To return to the topic of this research, we feel that the development of this notion in a manager implies a maturity in the acceptance of

goals and responsibilities, as well as a dose of realism about objectives. Additionally, this manager accepts that work is one more aspect of life, and knows how much the job can ask of her in relation to her children, partner, leisure time or other non-work-related priorities.

6
Life Cycle and Types of Women Managers

Theories on the life cycle

In an attempt to develop a hermeneutic to help define the wide range of female and male identities in the world of upper management, we created four areas of analysis corresponding to their predominant feelings. In reality there is nobody who corresponds wholly to one of these models, but depending on the stage in the life cycle and the complexity of the organizational network, a female manager may feel closer to one model or another, depending on circumstance.

Throughout our research, we observed the existence of a common awareness in all the women that went beyond the variables of age, culture or social class. Let us recall that age plays a predominant role in this study, where we created a group of women between 30 and 45 and another group between 46 and 60, whereas men are grouped indistinctly in the 30 to 60 category. In the existing literature on upper management, especially when it comes to women, this variable is rarely included as a factor that might explain the differences, the degree of job satisfaction and the difficulty of reconciling work and family, especially at periods in life when maximum professional demands and maximum personal demands (small children) meet, that is to say, around the age of 30.

In order to explain these behaviors, we turned to organizational and group behavior theories, to gender sociology[24] and the sociology of work relations and networks, as well as to some writings on psychology and upper management. We included authors such as

Kets de Vries,[25] Clayton Alderfer[26] for intergroup dynamics, Félix Requena Santos,[27] Faustino Miguélez,[28] Charles Perrow,[29] Clara Coria[30] for the female life cycle, García Ferrando[31] for sports, Naomi Wolf[32] for issues of beauty and power in women, as well as writings on the Tavistock model among others. The combination of these different viewpoints enabled us to unearth elements that influence the degree of satisfaction felt at each period in the life cycle.

The life cycle is an insufficiently studied aspect of the social sciences literature. The first student of the life cycle was Sigmund Freud (1856–1939), who analyzed the development of personality, especially in childhood, and its profound influences on adult life. Later, Carl Jung (1875–1961) concluded that Freud had focused too much on childhood and internal psychological problems. His own focus was more on middle age and the influences from various social institutions, as well as from religion and mythology. He tried to bring together the interrelationships between the inner and outer forces.

Jung considered that the young adult was trapped between the conflicts of childhood and the current pressure from family and organizations, and that real change occurred with maturity, around the age of 40.

Erik Erikson was another scholar who explored this topic in his classic book *Childhood and Society*. His work creates a link between Freud and Jung. But available literature offers a limited concept of the life cycle.

According to Levinson,[33] the term "life cycle" makes reference to a particular sequence that he calls "seasons" in men's lives. Each period is different from the previous one, but at the same time there are constant elements. Metaphorically, he makes analogies between the seasons in a year and the periods in the life cycle. No season is more important than any other, but they need to be understood in their entirety. Sheehy[34] also tackled the issue of the male life cycle. With this approach, we will now broach the analysis of men and women managers and their transition to upper management positions.

Types of women managers: the competitive manager

From a general perspective we can find four broad types of female managers, some depending on age. The first two are the competitive manager and the integrated manager. The others we termed the

reactive manager, who projects all her problems outside of herself due to her personality, not her age, and the proactive manager who, upon seeing a difficulty, tries to revert the situation. This does not mean that there cannot be any more differences in managing style, nor that age conditions everything else. It is simply a first qualitative phase that enables us to have a global vision of the female problem as a whole.

The competitive manager is found among the younger women in our group, the ones who are between 30 and 45 years old. At the personal level, increasingly they are singles. Professionally, this moment corresponds with internal access and promotion within the firm. This is also the time when they think about motherhood, if that was a goal in their minds. It is a period of great expectations that will soon clash against reality, underscoring the difference between their wishes and the real possibilities of carrying them out. These first few years can be characterized by great effort and disappointment due to this realization of the real world's limitations on their ambitions.

This can be explained by the fact that both men and women enter a firm with unrealistic expectations about the possibilities for self-fulfillment and promotion at work, as well as the possibilities of reconciling work and their private life.

At this stage, the firm tests its new members with a kind of "social Darwinism," a selection system where only the ablest survive, or else those who display complete dedication. That is to say, there are no time limits or limits on the number of tasks that they should take on. Pressure is at a high during this period, and is added to the pressures of the hypervelocity society.

This moment constitutes the first struggle against reality, where gender differences and identity issues become clearer. For women, as we said earlier, this coincides with her period of greatest fertility, the best moment for motherhood, which could entail career discontinuity. This occurs simultaneously with her moment of take-off at work, which sometimes turns instead into a landing.

Men have no biological impediments and can continue on a linear plane in their career development. In fact we observed, in a majority of male comments, that the issue of reconciling work and family is purely a woman's problem and none of their own. After all, it is women who are faced with the dilemma of choosing, or on

fewer occasions, reconciling. This dichotomy is a fallacy created by a cliché that tells us that maternity demands 100 percent dedication for life, when the reality is that total dedication is only required for a limited period of time.

This contemporary fiction offers a vision of childhood that requires eternal maternal supervision. It is also true, says Naomi Wolf,[35] that motherhood is one of the moments of greatest tension for a woman, both biologically and psychologically. Her dedication is complete, whereas her preparedness is usually nonexistent. Added to this is the social pressure from work in the form of likely reprisals, either before or after the woman has fulfilled her reproductive role. This social stereotype keeps alive all sorts of confusion and hinders a solution to the dilemma.

On the other hand, as Touraine,[36] Giddens,[37] Covey[38] and others point out, we live in a period of decomposing social frameworks, where the individual and individualism are the winners. This, according to Touraine, determines the existence of a weak and changing "I" who is subjected to mass culture. In this age range we observe little gender solidarity and a scant feeling of belonging to a group, making the person dissolve and increasingly become part of the system.

This scant gender solidarity is reinforced by the "beauty myth." Women who aspire to higher management must make this myth theirs. The system is based on a "sexual selection" and beauty is common currency, says Wolf, as much as the gold standard is. These measures are socially imposed, and constitute an expression of social power that throw women into a fierce competition. These are imperatives that affect women, not men.

The beauty myth has no historical or biological basis. It rules over both appearance and behavior, and makes women compete against each other – divided, they shall never conquer. Since women have become stronger materially, they must be weakened psychologically – this appears to be the reasoning in current society.

Besides, powerful industries need to be held up, especially those dealing in cosmetics, diets and plastic surgery that help us maintain the myth of eternal youth. The myth of "corporate beauty" awards women the same kind of power that money grants men.

An additional element to this myth is that women are permanently seeking approval, which makes them vulnerable because

they place their self-esteem in the hands of others. The beauty myth is today more deceptive than ever, and creates a real neurosis in women struggling to live up to it.

Female individualism cannot be simply explained in terms of gender. Giddens points out that it is a modern trend because it involves establishing a distance with social functions, as we will see from the statements of some interviewees and participants in group discussions.

> I don't think they are obstacles, but rather options. No matter what a man says, he is much less concerned about the family and he doesn't think he needs to show the same kind of dedication to it. I think it's a personal choice, because it's true that being in a firm requires giving up a lot of things, and the more responsibilities you have, the more things you give up. (Manager, 44 years old)

At the same time, young women in the workplace are often seen as objects of sexual desire, and sometimes they become the victims of that situation. Many male managers are uncomfortable working under a female boss. But older women get more respect as professionals, because beauty is relegated to a secondary spot and their skills are valued instead. One example of this is the arrival of middle-aged women to positions of power such as the new president of Chile, Michelle Bachelet, Germany's Angela Merkel, Ségoléne Royal's near access to the French presidency and Hillary Clinton's run for the White House in the United States.

> Female managers act like men. There are women who don't know how to handle men, they try to set absurd limits because we are all colleagues. There are men who use one register when talking to you and a different one when talking to a female colleague. When I talk to a woman colleague I am not thinking: she's a woman, look at her body...I have never sought sex at work. If you mix sex and work, that's bad news. (Male manager, 37 years old)

This comment makes reference to the difficulties faced by women to maintain their authority in the workplace, striving to be different from men while keeping their feminine traits. On the other hand, it

seems likely that in the higher rungs of the corporation, and depending on the shortage of top positions, rivalry and competitiveness may emerge as part of the power games at these levels. We heard women who clearly opted out of this game, and others who simply considered them strategies, on their road to the top.

> There are fewer positions at the top, and many people who want them. It's not worth it. That kind of success means leaving many people in the lurch and in the end what we women want is for everyone to love us and for everything to be harmonious. (Manager, 42 years old)

There is a trait that shows up repeatedly in women, more so than in men, and that is the spirit of renunciation. "The need to be loved and approved by others is the backdrop and the explanation for this behavior." Men, on the other hand, do not seek approval but power, which is an indirect way of getting respect.[39]

The group of younger women claim their rights by strongly competing against the men. They need to be recognized as good professionals. Older women do too, but their strategies were different. Competitive managers rebel more against their families but not against society, which is what the previous generation did.

When asked, men constantly question this competitiveness that is so typical of modern corporations. Men compete without a second thought, but it really catches their eye when they observe the same behavior in their female colleagues.

This group of competitive workers fits the modern profile of Spanish female managers who are not very old but have left their most youthful days behind. These women appear to be caught in a dead-end street. They are trapped in the role of the perfect woman who works in a highly demanding environment, can deal with the challenges of the couple and with family life, and naturally has not given up the ideals of contemporary beauty: she is fit, healthy, slim, independent and so on. In a certain way there is a sort of self-delusion about the changing role of women in a global society, who seek to gain independence but without prioritizing any of the other roles assigned to her. We observe a predominance of the omni-potent style, a notion of the Mediterranean superwoman who thinks she can handle everything, who embraces the ideals of the social

and corporate image,[40] who is healthy, slim, in shape,[41] and is unable to visualize her own limitations.

They want to be mothers, although they postpone this for quite a while and "are scared of being trapped by their biological clock." They wish to be good friends, colleagues, directors, to be competitive, to look good, but there are only 24 hours in a day...these are great ambitions that keep young women enslaved for the sake of an ideal that is difficult to achieve, and all of it comes with low tolerance levels for frustration and overwhelming feelings of anxiety towards unforeseen situations or situations that require a strong commitment and display of power.

> I am very stressed, I am always running around, Mondays are always hard. We have team meetings in the afternoon...we need to slow down, because you get yourself into a spiral that it's hard to get out of. Sometimes I feel guilty for taking a break. Often you make plans with unrealistic goals. I am always looking at my Outlook agenda, and I can't live without my Palm [Pilot electronic agenda]. I am addicted to words, I check my mail, I delete mail...On Fridays I have to pull myself away from the computer. (Manager, 33 years old)

The new female manager is full of confusion and contradictions. She knows how to enforce her will, but often she does so with a bad conscience. Even if she seems immutable from the outside, the conflicts are raging on the inside, and this is clearly reflected by one of the members of the group meeting when she says:

> My closet is a mess, but I don't care. Clearly this untidiness makes reference to the inner world, which we don't pay much attention to. (Manager, 34 years old)

The new woman wants to be liked, makes efforts to please everyone, and this makes her fall into the dependence game. She wants to assert herself without hurting anyone, to reach her goals without trampling on other people, to convince without manipulating, to appear sure of herself. But her insecurities surface in her gestures, in her body language, in latent aspects, in the emotional tide that grips

her on occasions when she needs to take the reins of upper management and display her own power. Taken to extremes, it appears that identification models are sometimes taken from the media, where women are shown as all-powerful but always complacent and subjected to mass culture. The young female manager is nothing more than a screen on which to project the desires, the needs, the imaginary worlds created by the new communication and beauty industries.[42]

Women try to fulfill all the obligations of their various roles, and make sacrifices without expecting gratitude in return. All this makes for more anxiety and depression than men.[43] They start off under the assumption that they need to perform better than men in order to achieve more modest results. And indeed, they make more efforts but do not receive greater pay, nor are they valued according to their performance – they themselves are least likely to recognize their own merits. Some help their male colleagues by taking on the most thankless tasks, while the men do not hesitate to take on the most promising jobs or take the time to develop their networks. One of the male interviewees said:

> Women work better in the services area, where they can be independent at a small scale. Serving others is part of their nature...
> (Male manager, 42 years old)

No doubt this "attitude of service" can be interpreted in more than one way. This study aims to analyze underlying issues in order to detect and understand the true depth of change. The question would be "What does it mean to be a woman manager in a global society?" and "How to reconcile and prioritize at each stage in life?"

According to Coria,[44] we have developed a "ball metaphor," meaning that the main role of women has been to assist other people's games instead of their own. Coria holds that even if women are accessing jobs traditionally held by men, this does not change their existential position. Women, she says, are advancing "against the tide" and she proposes a change in the game. There are differences in social context. In northern and Anglo societies, women make a choice between their personal and their professional lives. In this age range, we can see the difficulty of integrating the

various roles, prioritizing different dimensions of their identities. The cost and effort of this independence are reflected in their comments. There are many quotes relating to this issue that emerged during the group dynamics for this age range:

> This is the first time that I set up a company, and nobody can prepare you for it. A colleague resigned because she has a tumor, and everyone was crying. I am always stressed, and if you have any energy left you take on eight more things. And I don't even have kids or a husband. (Manager, 34 years old)

Once again, we are witness to the experience of hypervelocity, the emotional overflow and the scant awareness of one's own limits, of the inexorable passage of time. We perceive the lack of space within the company, or outside of it, to stop and think and emotionally process what is going on. The lack of children becomes manifest in feelings of loneliness and social helplessness by an ever wider spectrum of society.

> I focused on my career too much. Now I want to have a family but I am no longer 20 years old. There was no time when I consciously told myself: "I am giving this up." The years went by so fast, and suddenly I find myself alone... (Manager, 40 years old)

Although for many this is a premeditated decision, for those caught up in the latter situation there are clear effects, because European society still values the family very highly and the loneliness of modern society is not as easy to deal with as it might seem.

> The personal side of it is harder for me than the professional side. For those of us who are alone...everything requires your attention 100 percent. Nobody takes care of singles. I can't have dinner at home if I haven't previously bought the groceries myself. We mustn't forget women's domestic organization, there could be worse things. (Consultant, 34 years old)

During the group dynamics, after listening to themselves and to others, there was a dialectical spiral where cooperation and also

comparisons emerged as to how best to deal with the challenges of work and daily life.

> If something is wrong, when you have kids, things multiply. My husband's job forces him to travel constantly on business. We were a team but now I am alone. There's something worse than a single woman's agenda: it's having three kids. Mine are five, three and two years old. Until last January, my husband traveled Monday through Friday. Having an assistant at home is necessary. I work from nine to nine every day. I took this job because it is close to home. I am managing to survive...Now my husband works at his father's firm and he is home every day. He dresses them in the mornings. Before that, I had to take all three of them into the shower with me, I had no other choice. Now it's as though I'd gotten married all over again, and I am a lot more relaxed. (Manager, 34 years old)

One of the keys that constantly emerged was the need to plan time efficiently – weekly and monthly planning in order to achieve results (S. Covey).[45] Sometimes women get so caught up in their many tasks that they do not stop to think whether what they are doing truly matters. The need to plan appears as an antidote to lack of control and overflowing emotions.

> I am a very organized person. I have time for everything; I always set priorities. I see my children from seven to nine in the morning. I spend many hours at work – I don't work a lot, but I talk a lot. My job is not stressing, and time flies by. It is essential to be disciplined in order to survive. You have to learn how to say no. We create many of our own obligations. (Manager, 34 years old)

On this point, men and women differ considerably. Despite being super-demanding on herself, a woman is more aware of her own limitations and is better disposed towards giving things up, which is a sign of more emotional maturity but also, in the words of C. Tobio,[46] it can be a mistake because it leaves control in the hands of others, leaving one's own worth to one side.

The works of the French psychologist Françoise Dolto[47] under-score the importance of saying no to the kids, to set limits that develop tolerance to frustration, which is synonymous with psychological maturity.

> We get caught up in the discipline of goal-setting. We have too much stress to create any more goals for ourselves. We are in touch with many people every day: if it used to be ten, now it's a hundred. I am completely exhausted. When I don't meet my deadlines I feel guilty, I always have the feeling that "I have to," never the feeling that "I want to." If I can't deal with everything, I feel guilty... (Manager, 36 years old)

Besides feeling guilty for not being able to reach all the pre-established goals, there is another fear: that of not being sufficiently feminine, of not living up to the ideals of beauty and play all the expected roles. Male colleagues say that "women managers are not sufficiently feminine." If a female manager sees little of her husband because of work requirements, she knows she is not fulfilling her role as an ideal wife and mother. When she doesn't tell her mother that she is meeting friends, she is hiding the fact that she is not playing the role of dutiful daughter who must always have other people's priorities foremost in her mind. At the same time she seems incapable of identifying her own desires.

When she works with other women she feels less pressure and more understanding. Research into nonverbal communication shows that women sustain other people's gazes, but look away when the other person seems uncomfortable. They seek supports to know how to act, and after a brief look they check to see that everything is all right. It could be an attempt to soothe or to seek approval. In reference to this feeling, one interviewee said:

> I am my own boss. I am doing well now, I work mostly with women. I went through two periods. Working with men reminds you that you are a woman. Now I feels as though I had removed my corset, there is less pressure...It's a much more relaxed work atmosphere. When you work with men, through nonverbal communication they remind you that you are different. When you go

to a café, the men are all there, sitting in a corner... (Manager, 42 years old)

If you are a young woman, you are reminded that you are an object of desire,[48] that you are different...Managing sexual attraction in hierarchical structures can be a problem. Organizations facilitate the dynamics of attraction by providing an environment where goals create common interests. Close contact means frequent interaction, and daily transactions pave the way for social and sexual exchange. Sexuality is rarely left outside the workplace, and situations can arise where it becomes difficult to manage. The daily news provides ample coverage of situations of psychological harassment at work. Sexuality in the workplace is a stress factor, especially for female junior managers.

According to Sarrió,[49] sexual harassment is another manifestation of a patriarchal culture, which is reflected in organizations. The consequences for those who suffer it are diverse, ranging from quitting their jobs to requesting a transfer, or taking leave for depression, anxiety, stress and other psychosomatic symptoms that conceal a history of sexual harassment or a sexist work environment.

Sarrió talks about the use of language; discourse and images inside organizations are loaded, either manifestly or in a latent way, with expressions that tend to make female competition invisible and attempt to perpetuate the division of gender roles and sexist clichés attached to them. Proof of this is the comment by French politician Laurent Fabius when her party colleague Ségolène Royal announced her candidacy: "Who will take care of the children?" He was of course ignoring the fact that at 53 years old, Royal's "children" are no longer babies but mature people who do not require the attentions of a newborn.

The transition to upper management, as well as a shift in expectations, have led to changes in upward social mobility within organizations.

Men and women have been socialized in different ways. While the men are aggressive, competitive and assertive, women are more concerned about interpersonal relationships. This different socialization from childhood, which we will refer to again later on, makes it possible for men to be more successful in upper management even as they kill off the possibilities for women who might like to follow

down the same road. While women are more attuned to acceptance and relationships, men are more concerned about showing their authority, and instead of seeking approval, they wish to impress others.

> I benefited from positive discrimination, they were only looking for women at the gym. I was lucky. The other job was at a place full of men and I had a pretty tough time. There was a 55 year-old Arab man and he gave me a really hard time. Now I am happy because I am doing my job better. I think the fact of having children makes me get closer to people, they see me more as a mother. (Manager, 34 years old)

Women are more geared towards listening and this makes them get closer to people. They are less focused than men on competition, whereas male managers are deathly afraid of failure. The presence of sexuality in the workplace, present though silenced, can be a factor that explains the existing ambivalence over affirmative action or female quotas inside a firm.

Among female interviewees, some said they had to act as their mothers' mothers, that is to say, they had to make up their own models because the ones they had were not satisfactory. This happens with mothers who make their daughters take on the role of adults that they cannot assume themselves, thus creating a double pressure for the daughter.

> I was the eldest of four sisters, my mother was always depressed or absent, and I had to take care of everything. I did so just to prevent our mother from causing a scene. I needed tools for survival. I was basically never afraid. I've been doing things I didn't really know how to do for zillions of years now. My grandmother kept telling me: "Aren't you ashamed not cleaning up around here?" I seek a balance through my skills. Sometimes I am perceived as a masculine woman. The message was "look out for yourself." (Manager, 34 years old)

What we see here is a lack of female-emotional identification models, a mother who is there, who helps her daughter mature at all levels. We also observe difficulties in the negotiation process that

Table 6.1 Mother-Daughter Bonds

Healthy bond	Unhealthy bond
• Bond of protection and security • Helps daughter grow and fly on her own • Does not project problems on her daughter • Does not compete over age • Encourages daughter's growth and is glad to see it • Positive relationship between adults • Mother with problems	• Trapped in a tense relationship • Generates frustration and anger in daughter • Projects her frustrations from past hardships on the daughter • Mother and daughter cannot differentiate • Mother with problems • Difficult relationship • Hinders emotional growth

Source: Produced by author

can occur on three levels: asserting oneself, yielding to others, or negotiating. In the previous comment we can see an element that is present in many women, and that is the act of yielding in order to appease others, of putting other people's desires ahead of one's own, be they your mother, your partner or your children, just to "prevent a scene." In this way, one's own wishes are postponed time and again. Loneliness also encourages a proactive attitude, a behavior that is not conditioned by age or gender. "The message was look out for yourself." Placing demands on oneself is something that shows up at nearly all levels – work, personal, emotional. A healthy mother who has adequately journeyed across all periods of life can assist her daughter through the same process.

It is apparent that there is no clear-cut female workplace identity, except in contrast to the male model, which is often imitated. In almost all the interviews there was very little identification with the mother figure, whether professionally or emotionally. Since time immemorial men have had a well-defined role in society, whereas women have to make it up. Nevertheless women have a great advantage: they can choose, whereas men are "trapped in the imperative of production."

We choose at all times, we have that option, we are our own barriers because we always want more. If a woman is the boss she is worse than a man, because you replicate what you criticize. It pays to have a high position, I think we still have a lot of

pending issues...In short, we choose to live in three dimensions, not just one. (Manager, 39 years old)

This is also a period of exploration where women try to combine the personal and professional sides of their life. With time, positions become more flexible, the first achievements and recognitions make people more satisfied with their jobs during this period. Time goes by and it seems like one has found his or her place in the world. The family and kids take up space in managers' minds, in their distribution of time and in their energy. While for women their career projects collide with their personal projects, for men this is the time of professional take-off.

A final note on this group: It would seem that they constantly need to have men's approval. They *are* inasmuch as they fulfill the other's ideal. It is as though they had not developed their own ideals, as if fear or guilt were the predominant factors. Fear in female interviewees emerged as a paralyzing force. They tend not to verbalize their fears, nor can these fears be seen as having beneficial effects, like a red light telling us where to be more careful or where to come to a halt. Fears usually have a domino effect, triggering a series of negative thoughts about what can happen if this or that decision is made. By not differentiating the facts that simply happen, such as the passage of time, accidents or climate change, from the fears that can be managed through proactive action, the fear remains. In female managers, fear appears more diffuse, hard to apprehend, and is manifested in a difficulty to break bonds and a fear of rejection.

Outwardly they will say that they are not afraid of anything, although some admit they are scared of being lonely, of not being loved, of being abandoned. For those who have not broken out of the pattern, there is the fear of damaging their emotional bonds. The dichotomy work-family appears as a nearly constant issue. Reconciling schedules, which is little more than an attempt at accommodating external factors, leaves internal structures intact – that is to say, not breaking with the established pattern.[50]

The integrated manager

This is a type of woman who is comfortable with her own identity and her personal and professional development. They are women

who feel like they have "fulfilled their duties." Those who have had children are now past the age of greatest demand on them as mothers and the age of acting as satellites of other people. This group of women feel good about themselves; they have found a balance between their own demands and the demands of their environment. The wisdom and experience conferred by age allows them to observe their own evolution from a certain distance. They have taken risks, they have been mothers and they have enjoyed and experienced motherhood. They have learnt from practice. They know that risk can mean winning or losing.

They have focused on their own road, on their immediate circle of influence, not on worries and concerns,[51] and without deluding themselves about their image as reflected back by their immediate surroundings. They also do not feel the pressure of the "beauty myth," or worry about their age – they have moved beyond the sexuality that could interfere with their career development. They are respected because of their age and their accumulated experience. They are the women who reach power in politics and company boards. They believe in their own abilities to reach their goals. They are fulfilled, independently of whether their personal lives ended in divorce or not.

Having clear ideas about their goals is reflected in a greater independence and an increased will to live. Those who have decided to take a risk, and have done so, are not afraid of defeat. They know that it is part of life's road, and that a misstep does not constitute failure. They know how to convert stones into steps.

These women do not allow their plans to be thwarted because of a "no" or a wrong move. They don't take "no" personally. If things do not turn out as planned, they analyze the situation in a constructive manner. They are women whose predominant trait is a character ethic, not a personality ethic. They don't waste time looking for their own faults, instead they think of creative solutions, and this personal and organizational behavior paves the way for personal autonomy. They have worked the skin off their bones to break past the glass ceiling. It is also true that they have not felt the pressure of hypervelocity or globalized society. At this point they look back on their lives with peace of mind, even if many of them feel that their nest is empty. Their apparently lower ambition is a result of their wish to develop several aspects of their lives. This fact limited their

promotion possibilities, but it also gave them an inner strength that sets them apart significantly from women who belong to other age groups. Their ambition was fundamentally to clear the road ahead of them.

This is the predominant feeling among women aged 46 to 60. We call them "integrated" because they were able to reconcile several aspects of their lives: as career professionals, as women, as wives, as mothers, as daughters. They have a strong sense of group solidarity, because they are the women of the democratic transition who value women as a group and say that they always have a good time when they are around other women. In their own words, they feel at ease and can be themselves without the need for approval, as we can see from the following comments:

> I hadn't felt this good in years. Sometimes they put pebbles and stones in my way. A colleague of mine left and I was told that I was the best boss she had had in her life. Sometimes I am asked why I feel so good about myself. It's because I am free from a lot of bonds, and I can say what I think. I've recovered friendships from 30 years ago. I have great freedom, serenity and maturity. (Manager, 57 years old)

> I've suffered a lot. I am separated and have a hyperactive child. Self-control helped me a lot. Children require patience and self-sacrifice, and I have problems with the eldest one. Difficulties can be turned into something positive. Having my own company provides a great degree of freedom. (Manager, 46 years old)

The older women have already been through midlife crisis, a time when both men and women become increasingly aware of time constraints. They think more about investing positively in what's left of their time.

> I love taking risks and making decisions. The worst moment I went through is when my husband left me. He was with another woman and they had a child together. He emptied out the bank accounts, and my two children and I were left out in the cold. I had left my job, but I went back to see them and ask if they would take me back, even as a cleaner. They told me they needed

a director general, and by the following Friday I was part of the board. (Manager, 58 years old)

We can see that the cliché that holds that women are more averse to risk is false, at least in terms of vital attitude. It could be that this aversion is limited to material matters, for which they have not been properly socialized.

It is easy to observe from these comments a fighting spirit when faced with the need to provide for their children, and a capacity for swallowing their pride and begging if need be. There is a new vision of time: "Life is restructured around what is left to live, instead of what already happened." Another way of looking at it is from one's personal vantage point: practical knowledge or stagnation. In the business world, the manager can encourage the younger workers' development and become their mentor. Or, on the contrary, the manager can remain within the "comfort zone," marked by a lack of growth that gives rise to envy and bitterness over lost opportunities. The mentor figure appears more often in men as a key factor to promotion, whereas for women it is more a question of needing to feel support in their career path. The awareness of time and limits is given by age and motherhood as they watch their children develop and grow.

I am 49. I spent 20 years as a student, and became a mother at 40. Because I am now 49 I have my priorities straight regarding what I want and what I'm capable of, and I am very relaxed about it. I had a little girl late in life, and the child is the hardest part. She is eight now. (Manager, 49 years old)

This is the moment when the bottleneck represented by the organization is perceived most clearly, and women become aware that moving up the hierarchy has very limited possibilities. Progress will be slower or will stop altogether, with the resulting sense of deterioration. This is sometimes made worse by a certain amount of physical deterioration (menopause), which could combine with a period when conjugal satisfaction is at an all-time low, ending in many divorces. This moment implies accepting the limits of life and the disparity between ambition and achievement.

We don't give up things that make us happy just because of work. Personal life is more important to us than it is to men.

We have certain advantages after the age of 60. Our self-esteem is high…the information economy allows for greater flexibility. There will be more online courses. Everyone will be active. You can manage your time any way you like. Flexibility is part of freedom. (Manager, 49 years old)

Another important factor for women is the new technology. The cell phone is a great step forward for women, who can be yet not be somewhere at the same time. Even if you are at a meeting you can be located in case anything happens to the child. You can be connected to home. This gives you great freedom as a mother and as a professional. This is today's woman. (Manager, 59 years old)

In general, this age range is very optimistic. They make the most of their time. They are constant, persevering, and many of them fit into the category of "proactive." Their gaze is not passive, because if it was, their own lives would be alien to them.

They become the main characters and participants in their own lives. They have realistic criteria and see things the way they are, without delusions, seeking practical ways to face each moment. They admit that things have changed, even if this process is painful or hard. Acceptance simply means recognizing vital motion. To know that they have not been left "without a place," but to understand that due to the course of events, to fate or to whatever one wishes to call it, life has provided a different place for them.

I was recently widowed, and my mother also died recently. I used to be the queen of the house for my husband, my children, my mother. Now the kids are all grown up and I am no longer a queen. It's very hard for me to keep going, but you have to keep trying, building yourself up little by little… (Manager, 54 years old)

Women's networks are based more on bonds of affection than on bonds of utility. They positively value friendship and family, even if they haven't built a family of their own because they put their careers ahead, or because they just haven't found the right person.

I am happy about my life. I am not married, and I enjoy many sides of life. I have my family and my niece, whom I love as

though she were my own daughter. I have plenty of friends. When we talk about who fills your heart, we often forget about friends. I am more intimate with women; if I have a problem with my love life I always tell a woman, because I feel closer to her. (Manager, 58 years old)

To experience change with an open and flexible attitude means putting up with uncertainty and leaving known spaces and comfort areas behind in order to face new challenges that require courage. This is where we observed great differences between this group and the previous one, for whom time seems to slip away. They cannot stop to think, they have the "tired woman syndrome." The transition, however, enables them to appropriate these changes, to wade across them and incorporate them into their personality by adopting different attitudes. They know they are losing something, but it could also be the passport to discovering and developing new desires.

I have been dyeing my hair since I was 30. I am four years older than my husband. My family used to say "Don't worry, men age from one day to the next." (Manager, 49 years old)

My self-esteem is high. I started menopause at age 45. Menopause is my personal summer. (Manager, 47 years old)

During this period, women can have a double feeling that "time is running out", or on the contrary, that "new opportunities" are arising because they have fewer obligations towards others. Women become the main characters in their own lives, which they can observe calmly from a distance. They speak openly about the passage of time, about menopause, and about the biological, psychological and social changes this brings about. These women are satisfied with their lives, they feel fulfilled, and they can help liberate the potential of the younger women without entering into the competition game.

I have a daughter who is impressive at the professional level. She studied law and the stock market, then went to New York, where she lived and worked for three years. Then she spent two

years in Geneva and now she is in London. Things are going great for her, she travels all the time, she's seen the world. Now she's set up an orphanage in India, in Calcutta, with a Catalan friend who lives there. She is single, she doesn't have a boyfriend – well, she has one every three months. She is searching for balance, and says that in this material world she needs a spiritual space. (Manager, 56 years old)

These statements show a new kind of woman who is sure of herself, independent and self-reliant. She has discontinued relationships and balances competitiveness and material life, while developing a spiritual side. There is also a new kind of mother figure who is happy and proud of her own career path. From this spot they can admire and love their daughters without judging them for their desire to be different. But that can only happen when one is satisfied with one's own life and when personal self-esteem is high.

The great revolution for women came in the classroom, with coeducation. Equality began there. It turned out that the smartest student in class was a girl and that the top scorer at official examinations was a woman. I'm not saying that women are smarter, but they are more self-sacrificing. We are more practical, we know how to separate the wheat from the chaff and keep the essential. Men sometimes get lost, they turn things around and around. I don't know, maybe they're a bit less decisive. (Manager, 53 years old)

In their statements, women talk about the various paths and choices their generation had to make: getting married and socializing with other people for many, finding their own independence for others. Clearly there were different styles for conflict resolution based on gender.

Many women went to college to find a boyfriend, while others graduated but did not work. Many got married and left their jobs. I was very clear about the fact that I was going to work, although I wouldn't have minded staying at home and taking care of the kids when they were little. But I was afraid of going back to work in that case. I thought that if you quit, later it gets very hard to

come back. And that fear was stronger than anything else at the time. (Manager, 54 years old)

Often, women's path is defined in terms of struggle instead of viewing it as a journey of constant learning, not a gender issue but a question of attitude towards life.

It's not an issue of gender, but of your attitude to life. There are no doubt women who are extremely anxious to get to who-knows-where, and who don't care about balance, and there are men who are the same. There are phases in life, and perhaps at 40 you don't think the same way you do at 50. I think it's a matter of your attitude towards life. (Manager, 48 years old)

For many women of the transition, economic dependence on the man was not an option. They saw an opportunity to get training and take a different route from the preestablished one. Both at the intellectual and sexuality levels, they were liberated. Like one interviewee said, "the pill freed us from the man's pressure. We can decide whether to have a partner or not, whether to get pregnant or not, and of course we can enjoy our own sexuality."

It seems to me that people either were rich and could live off their family's wealth, or else they had to work. I could not imagine depending on someone else, to say "I'm going to marry and live off this man." I could not get my head around that. My mother did not work, but I had the chance to do so and I thought that was the best way. (Manager, 53 years old)

Most interviewees showed great clear-headedness, especially when it came to their options and how to put them into practice even if the environment was not necessarily favorable to change. With the transition, they accepted that "things were not like they used to be" and that the moment had come to "begin a new search" that included the construction of new spaces.

In order to take control of this period, they had to let go of the ones that came before it, to leave the past behind in historical terms and also in terms of age (menopause). They could not get change

and loss mixed up. From middle age onwards, these women took a different course, they fulfilled old desires that were incompatible with the roles they had to play when the children were little or the parents old. For integrated women, this age range is a second opportunity to develop old ideals. Men are not free from stereotypes either, but conditioning factors are different and their strategies for dealing with the passage of time are also different.

For women, conditioning factors are linked to three things: being satellites of others, being emotionally, legally or financially dependent on others, and finally, not thinking that motherhood is forever, but knowing that it requires greater intensity when the children are young. Being clear about this last point makes it possible to live more freely, and to see the period of the empty nest as an opportunity for greater autonomy rather than a period of loss and end of their roles as mothers.

As for the participants in the group discussions, they were aware at all times of their social and individual roles as sociohistorical transgressors. There are the women of the transition and they are the ones demanding an ever greater presence of women at all organizational levels, especially at the top. They develop networks of solidarity and female support, probably because they keenly remember the tough first moments of their own careers. They are satisfied with themselves.

In the 1970s these women took on positions of responsibility, both as mothers and within society, by facing up to the challenges of change all around them. These circumstances led them to be family, social and historical transgressors. Professional development allowed them to develop an identity in the broadest sense of the term. They feel a sort of gender affiliation that turned them into more integrated and whole individuals. At this period in time, when the children are no longer teenagers, women feel that they have "performed their duties" even if for a few, this new time on their hands is difficult to grasp.

> Now that my husband is no longer there, I don't have the obligations my mother used to have. I left my full-time job, and I have too much time on my hands. I am effectively more free now, but I don't know what to do with my time. For years I fulfilled the duties of a wife, daughter and mother. I kept running from one

Table 6.2   Emotional Maturity Continuum

Immature	Mature
Dependent	Independent
Passive	Active
Superficial	Deep
Short-term thinking	Long-term thinking
Subordinate positions	Accepting responsibilities
Projecting problems outside oneself	Taking charge of problems
Not developing personal power	Developing personal power
Little self-awareness	Keenly self-awareness

Source: Produced by author

place to another. Now I have all the time in the world, and I don't know what to do with it... (Manager, 54 years old)

We understand that the models of proactive or independent manager, or reactive and dependent manager, do not necessarily correspond with the models described in terms of age and gender. It's more like a personality structure. Integrated women, whose progress took place in adverse conditions, consolidated their personalities by advancing down a new road, turning into fighting women with a sense of perspective, and above all with clear ideas about what they wanted and what their life project was. Their role models were few, but many of them risked creating one of their own, which these days enables them to consolidate a more promising path. They are the ones who took risks and took the first steps, a process that is far from over. Society and its needs may change, but a good family bond is the prelude and the basis for building professional success. Table 6.2 differentiates between people who are emotionally mature and those who are immature, independently of their gender.

The proactive and the reactive manager

The proactive manager

Society advances, and women penetrate a world that used to be reserved for men – and vice versa, men are developing sides of themselves that used to be reserved for women. Proactivity is like a muscle, and it is achieved when one has moved from dependence to

independence and is able to relate to others in an interdependent way. They experience situations with a sense of optimism. These women are aware of the social transformation that is making them women of their time. Proactivity leads them to think and plan before acting. They are emotionally mature people who can think in the long-term and plan ahead to reach the goals inside their heads, both at the personal and professional levels. They have a high degree of self-awareness and feel capable of developing their powers and potential.

In the political arena, they have already reached power and left behind the fantasy of being rescued. They are no longer waiting for "the right moment," they just make things happen. There is a new feminism that is reconciling women with the pleasure of winning and the competitive spirit. Progressively, they are letting go of old inhibitions and knocking at the doors of power. If women are not able to make significant inroads in this century, to reach equality, it will be because they choose not to take that power, because power has been bestowed upon them naturally, it is a birthright. All the changes we are witnessing are leading to a change in image, they are small steps towards the construction of a new model of workplace identity.

> I work for the money. I used to believe in fulfillment at work. I would never set up my own company – let others be the ones to pay me... (Manager, 34 years old)

> I've been an entrepreneur all my life. I set up my first business at age ten, providing entertainment for children's parties, and I made a lot of dough. At 16 I set up a clothing factory in Argentina. I also studied architecture, although the only thing left from that period is my husband. When I saw how tough a career it was, I opted for business studies. (Manager, 46 years old)

These comments show the traits of the independent person, who can reach her goals and is determined enough to get what she wants. She does not fear power, nor a shift in roles inside the home. The new woman must never cease in her struggle, but she does so in a more elegant and intelligent manner. These days, women can achieve whatever they want.

I have a consulting firm. We work in human resources. We seek to develop companies and our philosophy is to encourage people to achieve their full potential. (Manager, 44 years old)

Emotional maturity does not necessarily go hand in hand with biological age. Sometimes, it is more closely related to one's experience and responsibilities in the course of life.

It's not just about getting a job, but about getting recognition. I have climbed over every barrier that I found along the way. I looked for investors and found them. Everyone told me it was impossible, to not even try, that I wouldn't get anywhere. But in the end you overcome all obstacles, whereas if you're inside a firm you don't. I looked for many alternatives before throwing in the towel. (Manager, 34 years old)

There are common traits among those who have succeeded: perseverance, clear goals, the ambition to fight for a promotion. Creativity and imagination seem to go hand in hand with women who can overcome obstacles.

I don't like limits, I am extremely bored by routine. If you saw the things we do in this company...when I set this up, my husband was really scared because he'd just been fired, I had left my own job, and we'd been told we were going to have twins...two kids at the same time, that's really something. (Manager, 46 years old)

Young, proactive women display a lack of limits, which can be read two ways: on the one hand, that all goals may be achieved, but on the other, that they have trouble prioritizing time and gauging their own strength.

According to Covey,[52] every task is performed twice. First you design the building, then you build it. This could symbolize the difference between simply working or actually planning one's life and career. These are not women who simply work, but who have developed a career plan.

There are two major obstacles: first, children. When they are grown up they stop being a problem, although later you have to

start caring for your ailing parents. Clearly these are barriers that the State should be resolving. There are also ethical limits, when you tell yourself "I won't do this because it is politically incorrect or illegal." And women feel that more deeply. Women are not as ready to go beyond the limits of ethics, while men are more open to the possibility. (Manager, 59 years old)

These statements show gender differences when it comes to principles ("I won't do this"), even if these decisions come at a cost.

Women take on many risks, especially for something they passionately believe in. New technologies, for instance, which at first seemed risky. Almost all technology companies in this country [Spain] are led by women: Microsoft, Hispasat, Google. (Manager, 55 years old)

I am skilled at rooting out talent. I am proud to be a woman. I feel more fulfilled than ever. I feel free to be heard. I am not afraid of others. I defend my ideas fearlessly. (Manager, 58 years old)

People ask me when I rest. I rest when I read something related to my career. I do not regret a thing because I am convinced that we are all whatever we want to be, and that everything we do we do for our own sake...I am stuck because I do what I like, and in the end that's a trap. For example, I wasn't able to go to the gym, which is the only thing I do for myself. (Manager, 44 years old)

We can see that women make choices and that everything has a price. In the case of this interviewee, she is coherent about her ambition but admits that she always leaves something behind along the way.

Nothing, not personally nor professionally. I have always been very balanced. I know up until when it's worth it to me, and when it isn't. Maybe that's why I am not a director general, but that wasn't part of my plan either. I like a middle-of-the-road place: a managing position but a significant private life as well. I want to have time of my own, even if you're always enslaved at

some point because of a client or something. Right now I simply could not be the director of a large firm. (Manager, 44 years old)

We can see that the same incentive gets completely different responses. One respondent said that she sacrifices part of her own time, while another said there are certain sacrifices she is not willing to make. It is clear to her that company time is set to a man's rhythm and that companies are mostly run by men. Time management shows up as a matter of concern at courses and seminars, and also in interviews. Company time is dehumanizing, enslaving, and unadapted to people who wish to grow as human beings.

> The work model, which is still dominated by men, is a waste of time. There are very long meetings that are called and then called off, where often people don't want to offer solutions so much as show off by delivering a speech. And the proof of that is that when women hold a meeting, everything gets solved in half an hour. We are much better organized, and that should enable us to have responsibilities within the firm and also have a life, which I do. I don't have any children but I have a private life and I like to lie on the sofa or go shopping. (Manager, 44 years old)

Time management emerges as a key issue. Reconciling work and personal life requires combining a compass with a clock. The main guidelines should be the principles that one of the interviewees made reference to. Women these days have the power to choose. Equality is no longer something to be begged for. In Spain, working hours are unlimited. Some women say that this is a strategy so that men won't have to share house chores, while others argue that it's just the result of bad planning. Economic studies indicate that Spaniards work longer hours and earn lower wages than the rest of the European Union. In any event, women make the case for the need to have more rational schedules that will allow them to reconcile work and family. It's not just a battle of the sexes, but a battle in a global society where pressure to be productive and pressure from shareholders is very strong.

> Men schedule meetings at six in the evening and stay until nine...If they schedule a meeting at seven, that's bad for me

because I have a child. Those are the three hours I spend with my little girl. I think they do it on purpose to avoid sharing responsibilities at home. In the world of sports or sports journalism it's always like that. It's all men, and I could swear they do it on purpose so they don't have to feed or bathe the kids, and then they get home when the child is already in bed and fast asleep... (Manager, 33 years old)

The reactive manager

Although it is not readily obvious in the interviewed women – they are managers – one could say that this attitude is present in specific areas of renunciation, and is latent throughout the study. Reactive women are basically dependent at the emotional level.

They have doubts about their own capacity to act successfully, and rarely achieve what they want. They can be placed in the emotionally immature category, as described in the previous table. They perform beneath their own possibilities and give up when they run into the first obstacle placed in their way. They are unable to turn stones into steps, lemon into lemonade. They lack perseverance, and that affects nearly all aspects of their lives. There are mental blockages tied to early learning experiences, to family messages heard over and over again that are etched into their mental software. These are women with a low self-esteem.

If a man or a woman always seeks to find faults within themselves and believe that these cannot be modified, then probably this thinking pattern was created by education. These people are convinced that things cannot be changed, that they are incapable of reaching goals on their own, and they also fail to establish solid bonds with others. These women fall into the category of "feminist victimism." Instead of opting for shared power, and enjoying the pleasures derived from it, they share vulnerability and an attitude of protest. They are ill-equipped to hold a position of power.

Among my college mates there are some who work in technology firms. The one who is at Indra continues to work there as a programmer. You can tell that she wants to be a mother, she doesn't want any complications, and she figures she wants to follow orders for the rest of her life. In the end it's clear that it's women

who choose to be mothers and often give up positions of more responsibility. (Manager, 44 years old)

Further proof of this emerged in the first group discussion, where women discussed, from varying points of view, the choice made by some of their friends to leave their jobs in order to raise a family.

It's always women who make sacrifices. Many women earn a lot less. When a child arrives, your career gets relegated to the back burner. And I think that's a mistake. (Manager, 39 years old)

We can observe the often-mentioned "mistake of renunciation",[53] the act of giving things up, of leaving life behind. In some way it is these choices, when they are not rectified, that make people feel trapped. Men can also feel trapped by the urge to produce, and they cannot always get out of these social traps.

Sometimes people are hired because of their profile. Women are very capable of being on company boards. I have seen many men who didn't open their mouths. The profile of the average manager is very low. There is a lot of resistance, but women are to blame. I have a friend who raised her children alone, another one stopped working because she lives of her husband. Some friends from school don't even remember why they married their husbands, they are unhappy, they are not working. There are decisions you make when you are around 20 years old. If you are married with three kids, how do you get out of that?... (Manager, 42 years old)

Some defend them, others criticize them, but at some point there is a moment of communion with earlier generations: everyone realizes that there is a link between them and their older colleagues. A group awareness is established, leading from an individual to a collective awareness. Some defend the right of a well-trained woman with a good job to choose to give it all up for the sake of her family, while the older women do not understand that and view it as an act of treason, as not honoring their own efforts in opening new roads for women.

But the most important part of the group dynamics is yet to take place. It is a short moment of silence when women recognize that they may have a choice, yet fear that this choice may amount to "throwing in the towel," to yielding to a frustration and weakness that any working woman experiences at some point in her life. In one way or another, these women are trapped in the web of dependence, or in a dichotomy between life, work and affection. Their low self-esteem has conditioned their life situation.

> Unfortunately, women are used to saying: "I'll sacrifice my job projection in favor of my husband and will stay at home to take care of the children." To me this is an unfortunate attitude, but I think this situation exists and it exists because women want it to. My sister is moving to Mexico because of her husband, and nowadays it shouldn't be this way. (Manager, 40 years old)

A situation of dependence sometimes makes it difficult for women to develop their full potential, even if they are financially independent. They may have money of their own, yet feel unauthorized to spend it. Sometimes the trouble lies in the fact that women feel they need to ask for permission rather than for simply an opinion. And this attitude places them in a position of submission instead of cooperation. Women with low self-esteem are reluctant to establish ties of solidarity or create networks with other women. There is a direct correlation between low self-esteem and low gender solidarity.

According to Coria,[54] in a patriarchal society "the mandate is for men to be independent and for women to be dependent – a dependence that is disguised as unconditional love." Coria adds that women feel vulnerable because they were taught that the protection they need does not come from within themselves, whereas men's socialization has always tended to show them that protection is found within themselves.

> I have a friend who worked like a mule, he paid for everything and she saved up, and in the end, they split up and she kept half of the company...I consider myself a feminist, but I look back and I think we are taking our revenge for our earlier inferiority. I think men are lost, confused, we haven't left them any space. I think women are more insufferable. Men have had their

security taken away from them, and during arguments they are despised for their inferiority. (Manager, 39 years old)

Elements such as frustration, disappointment, lack of recognition or equality compared with their male colleagues, absence of professional experience, leaving work to raise a family – these are all experienced negatively by all women at some point in their careers. There is another constant element among reactive or depressed women, and that is the fact that, due to their low self-esteem, their relationship with others is usually not good. They criticize other women and are reluctant to implement gender solidarity, a crucial element in the creation of support groups.

Life cycle and gender differences

Up until now we have considered exclusively the types of female managers and their organizational behavior according to age groups, presenting a global view of the situation. Now we will analyze similar cycles, but checking to see whether there are gender differences. Let us go back to the first questions of the in-depth interviews, which are aimed at exploring the beginnings of the person's career.

I graduated in contemporary history, but never worked in that field. I began preparing for an official examination for the position of administrative technician. After studying for six months I took the first examination, failed, and never went back. Three years later I opened an antiques shop, but dropped that project two and a half years later and began this other project. We're about to celebrate its 25th anniversary, we started in 1981. My daughter was not one year old yet... (Manager, 51 years old)

When I graduated I did what everyone else does: I sent resumes out like crazy. I was called in for an internship at a company and started working in their finance department. It was supposed to last three months, but it worked out and I was the only intern who stayed on. There were about 50 of us, so I was lucky. (Male manager, 37 years old)

We can see that age notwithstanding, there does not seem to be great differences in the period devoted to the job search.

> When I arrived in Spain I saw I would not be able to do things my way. I didn't have a strong calling either, so I went into business. I answered and they hired me. (Manager, 59 years old)

There is a very similar process when it comes to getting that first job. A proactive attitude conditions the results:

> I was 27 years old, and they hired me because my English was good. I had lived in the United States for seven years and spoke the language well, and I had a degree in science. When you have a science degree you have a great capacity for analysis and synthesis. Back then you needed all those qualities. (Manager, 52 years old)

The initial moves appear to focus on joining a firm to gain some experience, although there can also be more entrepreneurial characters who begin their professional lives on their own.

> Three friends got together, each one with different goals. I had been studying for official examinations, and it was hard to know what the different options were...There was the possibility of publishing a guide to help graduates understand their different options after leaving college. We published the first guide in 1981, and continued up until 1990. There were other options we were able to explore with computer technology. (Manager, 51 years old)

> I married very young, right after turning 23, and I had a daughter when I was 25. There were not many women of my generation who worked, at least there were few in Spain. There were not many married working women. (Manager, 53 years old)

Early on in a person's career, different elements emerge that condition personal choices. Whether men or women, one possibility is to try several options until some pleasant occupation is found.

Another possibility is to be entrepreneurial and launch a project until a team is consolidated and a niche found in the market. In other cases skills such as those provided by a science degree, or language skills – very much in demand both then and now – can be the determining factor. In any case, we cannot establish a common pattern, but simply list the options and watch how certain messages have conditioned personal choices.

There were only two of us (women) studying physics and three of us getting a doctor's degree in materials engineering: two American girls and myself. I never thought about gender issues, only about whether I liked the subject or not, whether I found it fun. Physics provides you with an intellectual background that few other degrees do, and that has been useful for everything else. (Manager, 59 years old)

We observed different strategies and moves depending on college training (humanities or sciences), as well as graduate degrees and periods spent abroad. Having gone through the first stages of motherhood is also a turning point when it comes to commitment to one's career.

My son was six years old, and Isabela was ten. My real professional development came when they were already going to school, and that was a very important moment for me. (Manager, 51 years old)

There is a differentiating element here, and that is the fact that whereas women's career development is marked by their children's evolution, most men's careers take off regardless of their family's evolution. Whereas we find similarities among young men and women, for the men the need to work and material concerns are well-defined from the first moments of the interview.

My career has little to do with my studies. Deciding what you want to be when you grow up is tough when you are not mature enough. I passed college entrance examinations and started studying medicine, but I thought: "I can't spend six full years without working." So the second year I went into nursing and

started working. I dropped medicine after realizing it was a mistake... (Male manager, 48 years old)

There is also a search for a strategy in terms of seeking professional development or establishing a career plan. This is a road that clearly points upwards. For women, workplace identity is less well-defined because they lack as many role models and because their trajectories are less well-defined. Not so many differences are observed early in their careers, however.

There is a crossroad in your life when you start touching on issues that you had not considered before, and you find that you like them, that you feel comfortable working with them, and you go into them more deeply. I felt really attracted by private corporations. I had an offer from the company where I work now, and that was 15 years ago. I started as a mid-level manager. Usually you start at the bottom, but I had management experience so I started out as a manager. (Male manager, 46 years old)

Another very different moment is middle age. After the first few years, expectations are compared with reality and people begin to realize what their situation is. Achievements are consolidated, and in the case of women, who have a smaller networking capital and less social support, their self-esteem begins to consolidate. Following is Nathaniel Branden's definition in his 1993 book *New Women*:

Positive self-esteem operates as an immune system for the spirit, providing resistance, strength, and above all a capacity for regeneration.

For our interviewees, self-esteem was reinforced by external factors that, in the long run, resulted in greater inner security. This self-esteem is acquired throughout life, especially at a younger age. People with high self-esteem are more willing to take risks, to accept new challenges. Women with high self-esteem know how to ask, those without do not.[55]

The first time I was on television I didn't tell anyone about it, just my father, because I knew it would make him very happy to

see his daughter on TV. The repercussion was huge. (Manager, 51 years old)

In this case, it was social recognition that provided this woman with personal security, confidence in her project and a chance for professional takeoff. Security in turn encourages creativity.

> It was a turning point...we realized that we had to explore different channels, that we were able to offer the entire college community a permanently updated service. From that moment on, we took off. (Manager, 51 years old)

Social recognition brings the need to obtain material compensation as well, a topic which is a taboo in our society, especially when those requesting compensation are women. Traditionally, women have not had a socialization in material matters, as opposed to men. Among women, there is sometimes a latent conflict between altruism – putting others ahead of themselves – and egoism – thinking of themselves first.

> That is when we started to make money, but our first employer was the University of Valladolid. They were our sponsors, they bought the entire program for employment and training...that must have cost them about five million, I think. With that money we were able to take off. (Manager, 51 years old)

> When you are a partner, you feel part of the company. It is a tough system where you have to be very demanding of people, but you set the ceiling. If you have a good disposition, a willingness to learn...in the end, life is not about what happens to you, but about how you react to what happens to you. You feel more responsible but also more satisfied. (Male manager, 48 years old)

We observed gender differences when it comes to securing a position. Women are more delicate, they take smaller steps. Men act tougher; exercising control and making requests are their predominant behavioral pattern. Women tend to band together, to do things without rushing into them, though without taking breaks either. The paradigms are different from the start. Until now,

women have hoped that their invisibility will make others be aware of their abilities. Men on the other hand tend to create the environment that will facilitate their success. They don't make a bigger effort, they just apply all their strength to one spot, being clear about the fact that they want to rise to the top. Women, as we gathered from all the interviews, are much more critical with themselves. They make much greater efforts to achieve the same results. Proactivity has little to do with gender or age, it's more an attitude towards life.

> In my case, I deliberately caused changes. Luck is a factor and you have to get lucky, but you also have to be in the right place, and you have to make that happen. To use the clover metaphor, you have to cultivate it even if it is unlikely to grow. There is always a certain amount of premeditation. First I started a career, I was a manager, then I moved to the world of academia. I was never afraid of change. (Male manager, 50 years old)

Mind rules over emotions. Men have been socialized not to externalize their feelings. Fear is made manifest in symptoms, illnesses, psychological reactions rather than a verbalization of their feelings. They are more action-oriented and less attuned to emotions. They are more focused on their own needs than on those of others – almost the opposite of women.

> I like to take the plunge. The main thing is your attitude towards life. You can achieve whatever you want. You set your own limits. If something doesn't work out, I try something else, but the main thing is to have a permanent learning attitude. It's hard to get along with people in an environment like this one, where competition rules. If you are weak, they'll tear you to pieces. (Male manager, 46 years old)

The transition to the upper echelons of a company requires a strong sense of involvement. Depending on age, one can adapt with greater ease to the job requirements. But even when a woman is willing to move and to organize her life around these requirements, it is companies themselves which, based on social clichés about women, decide to send to them abroad on fewer occasions, and

when they do so, to less developed countries.[56] Contact with diversity, with different ethnicities, cultures, ways of thinking, of negotiating, of doing business, are a key element for managers of 21st century corporations.

> I started working on a project for all of Spain. They were implementing a system that worked really well and asked me to travel with the team to several countries. I became an expert in financial processes. They were very good years, if very tiring ones. I traveled nearly every week. After a few years I asked my boss to let me slow down a bit and he sent me to the US. (Male manager, 37 years old)

> I try to make overnight trips at the most. What I do is, I go with my husband and daughter to the daycare center, and then I come here. That way I have three hours with her, plus weekends, which are intensive programs with the child. We never, ever go out for a drink or dinner…it's all about the child. (Manager, 33 years old)

Statements from either gender regarding expat life are quite different in terms of age and responsibilities. Women are increasingly assuming travel as part of their jobs, but with great limitations. In general terms, women managers are underrepresented in the international arena. Among the reasons for that difference is the fact that male bosses send them abroad less frequently due to prejudices about their allegedly lesser capacity to adapt to unknown environments. Another variable is that they are less present in selection processes. Specialized literature cites the fact that women managers have fewer informal networks than men, and so are not as frequently recommended for the job. In some countries there can also be some hostility towards female managers. Selection processes generally look for counterparts with whom to carry out a long-distance relationship, and given that there are few women managers, men get sent more often. In general we observed that women's statements nearly always included references to the family, whereas men do not appear to show the same concern over having to reconcile both roles, even if the family may be a destabilizing factor. The time variable, men's interpretation of absence, their feelings towards

separation are completely different from women's. For women, somehow or other, it is always about compensating for the guilty feeling of not living up to the social expectations of a woman who is a manager, a mother, a wife and a daughter.

7
A Man's Viewpoint: You Want to be like Goddesses

How they see themselves

A study on women in management positions could not omit the male viewpoint, given that this has always been, and continues to be, eminently a man's world. This viewpoint is in turn conditioned by several determining factors, the first of which is a matter of class. In Spain at least, upper managers come from the upper classes, which are mostly conservative. There is a second factor related to gender – which, in a way, is also a class issue.

Following the methodology set out in this study, ten interviews were conducted among a group of upper managers in the same age range as the women; there was also a group discussion among managers where age was not a discriminating factor, since the biological variable does not have the same influence on men as it does on women.

It was quite striking to observe the initial reactions of the men gathered there to talk about themselves and about their female colleagues. Unlike the women, who immediately began to communicate with each other by asking about jobs, personal lives, children and so on, the men displayed a certain discomfort. They asked for paper and pen to take notes, even though there was nothing to write down – they were there simply to talk. There were numerous comments about the air conditioning, whether they were getting any air, how the air was coming out of the vents, whether perhaps the air should be turned up... The scene was reminiscent of the opening debate in the film "12 Angry Men," where a group of male

jurors who don't know each other must deliberate the guilt or innocence of a man charged with murder. The air conditioning, in a way, represented the lack of psychological air caused by a situation where they felt trapped. There were also complaints about their clothing – they said that women have it easier because they do not have to wear a suit and tie. The men also talked about what happened to them on their way to the discussion group – arguments with the taxi driver and so on. These were informative comments, not personal ones, and were meant to break the ice.

In the course of the meeting there were no personal or work-related exchanges. It became clear that men have not been taught to ask questions that might even remotely delve into the lives of others; that is not part of their agenda. Only rarely do they evidence any kind of emotional crack. As a rule, everything is always going great and they do not feel the need to seek professional guidance unless disaster strikes. There is a body of research analyzing the frequency of visits to the doctor according to gender, and results show that men seek out health professionals much less often than women. And when they do, they do not ask questions. Nowadays, men over 40 feel that their playing field is radically different from their fathers'. This outlook on reality became clear when the men were asked how they felt at this particular period in their lives. Some replied:

I feel better than ever. I've been working for a long time and I usually make the most of it because I am passionate about my job.

I am thrilled to have been born; now I enjoy myself a lot more than I did when I was young. Personally, I have left behind a period of struggle. Nowadays I do what I like.

I am glad to have left college teaching behind. When I left, it was a traumatic situation, not a voluntary one. Now I am back in teaching, and I enjoy it very much. I don't have a wife or kids, and I greatly value friendship, being receptive, being able to give ...

I joined an expedition to Peru organized by a non-profit group, and that was very important for me. In the end you feel grateful

for what you have. We can be happy with just a few things. In 2002 I got married, and there were important life changes for me – marriage and kids. I think it's important to have a goal that is neither too radical nor too aggressive. The multinational I worked for had a big influence on me; lately I work as an independent professional ...

I am optimistic. As you grow older you enjoy each moment more, and you have a different perspective on things. Every day I get more pleasure out of doing things. Possibly I won't have time to do everything I want. Life is finite, and I am 59. You need to have a vision, a sense of where things are going, because we are all going to leave this world...

For this group participant, the notion of "limit," or the limited amount of time left for him to live, gives him a different perspective, a second maturity, which some authors place between 50 and 90 years of age. At this stage some men discover the joys of diversifying their roles instead of limiting themselves to the professional world, the public world. Now they wish to diversify their roles at the personal as well as professional level. They are discovering the joys of the emotional world, of leisure time. They are entering an age of wisdom that goes far beyond the momentary or material pleasure. Men who face this stage with a positive attitude can reap the benefits of the various lessons learned throughout the life cycle.

This is not a representative sample, people are usually not this happy. If you are a solid person, you can pull yourself together again and take advantage of negative situations. I am a religious person, I am coherent with my own beliefs. I want to be in charge of my life. The messages we get from our consumer society create a great dependence. A scared person is very easy to manipulate...

In this comment by a younger man, we can see a cross between the inner and outer worlds. There is a self-awareness and an awareness of the consequences of our consumer society. A society that sends out messages of fear creates citizens with a low self-esteem and lack of self-confidence, a fact that is ratified by the sentence "a scared

person is very easy to manipulate." Men do not exteriorize emotions, but women display fear and guilt, two worrisome aspects of the job of being a manager. Statements by female colleagues did not show such an idyllic personal situation. They felt free to talk both about their well-being and their discontent. One of them said "when I am in the presence of other women I feel like I can loosen up my corset." The communicating style was radically different for men and women. For the former, conversation showed few cracks or questions, few signs of a midlife crisis or of significant changes at some period in their lives.

> I feel more free these days. It's because of the ability to ponder what I am doing right now. I feel at peace, I haven't screwed up on any significant issues. I have worked for everything that I have, my freedom, sexuality, etc. Because I have worked so hard, now I have so much freedom, now I am getting some interest back.

"I haven't screwed up on any significant issues" hints at the emotional variable. It would appear that age brings with it a sense of peace. These men do not appear to be subjected to the era of hypervelocity that produces so much anxiety. Participants shared a sense of well-being with the older women – a sense of a job well done. There is a critical discourse about the multinational firm, as well as a need for freedom, for constant autonomy at work. Many statements were nuanced with a vocabulary relating to strategy, skills and tools used in their jobs – statements influenced by work. The words "strategy," "effort," "work," "I have worked for this" and "discipline" were heard often.

> The factors that had the greatest influence on me were effort and discipline...strategy and effort. Basically it's about attitude, about improving from an intellectual point of view. You have to aim high, because life cuts you down.

Again, we see a hint of some of the concerns men have, which are an addiction to work and the crisis created by an ever increasing unemployment rate, symbolized by the multiple mergers and acquisitions as well as early retirements. This is noticeable when the participant says "you have to aim high because life cuts you down."

We have the notion of ambition ("you have to aim high") and of direction ("effort and discipline"), as well as comparisons with the younger generations, the ethics of character as opposed to the ethics of personality,[57] of appearances, of a lack of fundamental values. According to the men who were interviewed for this study, this last trait is common among younger managers, whose main concern is to display a behavior more geared towards themselves than to others. They are narcissistic characters filled with an individualistic ethic.

The more you want, the greater the effort you have to put in. This is something that you do not observe among young people. Today it's top effort versus minimum effort. There are people who think a lot more about their leisure time. Values have changed. We didn't set the right example. The concept of work has changed completely, and I for one, demand the free time to lie down and do nothing.

We can see the contrast between two ethics, that of the maximum effort versus that of the minimum effort. There is also the ethics of the older man, who is aware of his own limitations, versus the young know-it-all executive, for whom the passage of time has not yet meant any significant life experience. There is also a contrast between economic security and a rising emotional security. The effort made by middle-aged men is apparent, as is the rivalry between different styles. In this confrontation, there is no reference to the female figure, nor to the double effort generally put in by women at work.

You go through university and university goes through you, otherwise you are a technician and nothing more. You are closer to the machine than to the man. Men value their time, machines don't. Time should be increasingly important, an essential issue, yet we tiptoe around it. The main thing is to have emotional balance.

Although on the surface everything is going well, there is a veiled fear of old age, of death, symbolized by the frequency of references to time. Men have not been socialized, at least for now, to express

their feelings. There is also a veiled reference to technology ("you are closer to the machine than to the man"), given that in real life robots and machines are replacing humans. Whereas women are defying the values and stereotypes in which they were raised, men at this historic moment and in this culture still need to break with the past in order to adapt to the 21st century. They need to be permanently updated and to adopt a different attitude because the rules of the game have changed. Now the head of a corporation can be a virtual boss, and all these transformations require a change in strategy and in attitude, as well as a nearly permanent coexistence with uncertainty.

Just as with women, family messages are fundamental as identification models for men, either to encourage or to repress them.

> I was very influenced by family role models, my mother for instance...My father was an engineer, my mother was the opposite. I am a therapist, and when you are fixing someone's mind, you need to be very intuitive. My mother gave me fundamental messages just with her presence, she loved me and cared for me...

In this particular case we see how the emotional variable of the female figure has influenced this participant, who only says about his father that he was an engineer. But when he talks about his mother he speaks of her attributes, her care, the way he felt loved by her, all of which are basic building blocks of personality. There is scant reference to the father, rather, the statement shows more of a "lack of a father" as a role model. There are references to basic principles that make up a vital compass, things such as mutual trust, useful behavioral models for professional life later on.

> The soul that drives a company is trust. People who take short-cuts are not worth it. Being honest has its own profitability, it is a sign of intelligence. Untouchable concepts are part of the human being. The opposite always ends up taking its toll...

When they talk about themselves, any difficulty is glossed over for the benefit of others. From the first, each man placed himself in a working group situation,[58] although there was a shift when the talk turned to women managers. The group began acting as a basic

assumption group,[59] that is to say, rather than thinking rationally, there was overwhelming emotion at the notion of women holding upper management positions. There was a transformation similar to that of Dr Jekyll and Mr Hyde. After the modern statements of the first few moments came primitive ideas about how feminine identity is based on motherhood, clearly without realizing that for women motherhood is no longer a priority. They considered all women managers as a homogenous group, without making any differences among individuals. There were no categories referring to either age, area of specialization, nor was there any awareness that motherhood requires different degrees of commitment according ito age.

How they see women managers

The first definition of identity is tied to motherhood, ignoring the gender variable and its cultural determinants. There is woman, period. We observed a great difficulty among men to create a mental picture of the female manager. On the one hand, there was little differentiation between the public and the private spheres. By stressing motherhood, this automatically became a limit on their professional development.

> For women, motherhood is the determining factor. The law protects that, and nowadays it has a contrary effect. I am a great admirer of women, they are very sensitive. A woman is like two men, or more. As a man I feel at a disadvantage, there are things that escape me.

The issue of motherhood as the only axis of female identity is repeated. There is a binary logic[60] that categorizes concepts in terms of "one or the other." Women accept this position from a situation of gender blindness. Being a mother is no longer the main goal for women. According to Burin,[61] around the age of 30 women undergo a crisis in relation to motherhood, whether they have a stable partner or not.

In this new place occupied by motherhood, which men seem not to have noticed, it is no longer so much a question of whether to have children or not, but about the fact that once children come,

they may be somewhat neglected, with the resulting early depriva-
tions. Especially among younger women, we find a generation
where mothers have cut back on their own role, yet fathers have not
taken over. Fathers' participation in raising their children is basic
because mothers no longer have unlimited availability.

The previous interviewee made reference to the increasing power
of women and the fear this produces when he said that "a women is
like two men, or more" and "I feel at a disadvantage." Also, if men
help more with childcare, new anxieties may arise that are interpreted as a loss of masculinity.

Women have defied the traditional patriarchal culture, questioning the values they were educated in, forcing a change in social,
family and workplace roles. Men for their part do not know how to
respond to these changes and feel displaced from a professional
point of view. Added to this is a change in their gender role, which
adds to their unease. Men are unable to visualize these changes as
new possibilities for personal growth, or for an opening up of roles.
They feel displaced and thus they feel like failures, which in turn
leads to feelings of vulnerability, of feeling "threatened." While
women underestimate their own power, men overestimate it.
Women do not see themselves as powerful and aggressive, even
when they are. They are not used to the weight of power. Men,
through their attacks on the female figure, appear defensive and
lost, because even if they don't lose their positions, they may lose
their centrality. This transitional period slowly produces a new type
of male behavior.

On the one hand we have the **egalitarians**, who defend the
necessity of change and enjoy using new skills. They try to learn the
new language and customs of this emerging world. On the other
hand we have the **traditionalists**, who decidedly resist change, and
see only loss in this transition. The statements we heard show that
male managers, both at the individual and group levels, tend to fall
into this latter category.

This latter vision, which is shared by many men and women, is in
contrast with a more egalitarian view of the world. It is just as sim-
plistic to think that all men oppose a more egalitarian society as to
think the opposite.

A salient feature of the group discussion was the difficulty displayed by men to talk about the social representation of women

managers. Asked about their opinion on them, men instinctively talked about women truck drivers, women plumbers, etc. as if they were unconsciously accusing them of trying to be like men. It is reminiscent of Faust's line in Goethe about wanting to be like gods. Included in this attitude is class contempt.

> The cards are handed out, and society puts you in the position of the warrior. It's a matter of dividing up the roles, and society sets out those roles for you. Families who live in the Amazon forest also have roles. The male hunter goes out to get the wild prey. The woman who cares for the children is playing an ancestral role. It is hard for a woman to demand being a gas canister deliverer. A third of women work in construction. They lift bricks like animals. There are also mail women. Everything is very technology-driven. In medicine there is only 50 percent of women. Women are ancestrally prepared to care for others. There is a lot of competition at the top, and men are better prepared for it...

Like we indicated earlier, the patriarchal attitude ignores changes and shows a lack of respect[62] and recognition of new realities where women are taking on leading roles where male protagonism is relegated to a second position.

At the same time, the rise of women constitutes a "threat" because this is no longer about sharing laundry chores, but about sharing economic power. While women underestimate their own power, men in practice fear women's advance. The key is not in whether women want to retain power, but in that they wish to share it in accordance with equality policies.

Men who fall under the category of "traditionalists" have still not listened to women as subjects with demands to make, and they do not recognize their independence. Women's arguments are not based on being the equals of men, and in fact their competitive edge lies in their difference. These statements reveal a series of contradictions that underscore men's difficulty to change places and rethink their own identities. We understand that behind this attitude of rejection lie fears such as:

1. <u>Fear of losing their privileges</u>, not just in the workplace but also at the personal level. The rich man does not want the poor man

to be like him. He has every right to, but if the poor man becomes rich, then the rich man stops being so, since he is only rich – with everything else that goes with it – as long as a poor man exists.

We must once again recall that men have been socialized to reinforce their professional side as a provider. This is their main role. Women, however, have been socialized in a diversity of roles, mainly oriented towards the private management of the home. That is why women's identity is multidimensional, whereas men's socialization is unidimensional as a provider.

There is no difference in gender, nor a clear differentiation between the public and private spheres; rather, confusion seems to prevail. In the men's statements, we see that if women rise in power, men automatically fall, or at least that is what emerges from their social imaginary, whereas in the real world access to the top is restricted and there are few spots available.

Women have extraordinary skills, but they lose them. Using those qualities the wrong way is something I can't see, they can be very favorable but the qualities are lost. They should not try to be like men...

Emotions flare up here through statements that women who use their skills lose them, and if they use other skills, men lose out as well, so that no matter what they do, women in the workplace will always meet with disapproval. The same goes for female associations or networks. These are reflections of a sexist culture. "Divide and conquer" appears to be the male motto. The underlying and unverbalized fear seems to be "if they unite, they will conquer us..." There is a feeling of unease in the face of a vague and confusing identity. By changing roles, automatically everyone else needs to change too.

Although women still will not admit to having power, men are afraid of losing it. All this results in statements on both sides that reflect the ambiguity of the roles men and women currently play.[63]

I think we are going through a very strange moment, because roles are changing. It's also hard for men, because we're still not

clear on what is expected of us, or what it is we have to do...
(Manager, 33 years old)

These statements show a feeling of confusion. If men have modified
their authority, they still maintain their situation of power.
Similarly, from a theory of complexity and a nonreductionist
approach, some women understand the behavior displayed by their
colleagues over the loss of their usual spot.

We are going through a period of change, and I think men are
under a lot of pressure. We also have our own kinds of pressure,
but they think they have to bring home the highest salary. In my
house, I have the biggest salary, I don't know whether it is a
question of ambition...they feel very responsible over the family
budget, and that may make them feel that their career is the
main thing. (Manager, 36 years old)

Nowadays, especially for younger men, issues such as the first job,
marriage and paternity have all become unpredictable. It's unclear
what they are supposed to do or when they should do it. It is at
once interesting and disconcerting, almost like sailing towards a
new world without knowing where you're going because the naviga-
tional charts and maps are obsolete.

Perhaps, although this may be confusing for women as well, the
first step might be to try to understand the stages that men are
going through, in order to learn how to navigate those changes in
the new masculine chart with greater awareness and a passport to
renovation in hand. Gail Sheehy[64] admits that after 20 years investi-
gating the impact of cultural transformation on both sexes, she concluded that men do not understand women, but at least they know
it. Women, on the other hand, do not understand men, but they
don't know it.

There are situations in which we might have had a confrontation
had I been a man, but with me they don't dare. There are some
women who get very hard, who seem resentful or bad. I have
always tried to negotiate, to make everyone come to an agree-
ment...we women have to fight a lot more...if a speech needs
to be made, men straight away sign up even if they don't know

anything about the topic. We are more about "No, you go ahead."
We're not as keen on standing out. (Manager, 44 years old)

Women admit there are managing differences among them. "Some women get very hard," "I always try to negotiate," "we women have to fight a lot more," "we may not make ourselves important." These comments show a reflection, a differentiation and a style that chooses to either stand out or to remain in the shadows.

Nowadays, for a woman to obtain a position of responsibility she needs to use a man's methods. In the end you need to use contacts the way they do. A man spends more time consolidating. While he is conducting an operation, he is also doing politics, both inside and outside the firm. We women don't do that so well. (Manager, 44 years old)

These comments reflect a certain amount of idealization with respect to men's abilities, and also clearly express the difficulties of developing networks. Several studies indicate[65] that men are more centrally-oriented and tend to create links with people of their same sex than women do.

Women have more support networks among their peers, whereas men have more utilitarian networks. When it comes to building these networks, men look more to professional experience in order to get in touch with key people, whereas women focus more on resolving momentary conflicts. Exclusion from informal networks is one of the main obstacles to women's rise to upper management. This means that those who have less insider information will have a harder time establishing strategic alliances or finding coaches and mentors. All these factors result in less occupational mobility and the effects of hitting the glass ceiling. While men spend more time negotiating, women spend that time working.

The patriarchal culture intends to maintain gender stereotypes linked to the creation of power networks and groups.

I know I am being politically incorrect. I am totally against female cabinets, even women's associations. I also disagree with quotas. Ten male ministers, ten female ministers, there can't be eleven...that is so stupid. If they can do their job, I don't care

whether they are men or women. Women are fighting for something they think they don't have. (Male manager, 42 years old)

There is a widespread notion that networks constitute a powerful mechanism to control and distribute resources. This informal interaction structure is rejected because it reflects the hierarchy and segregation of the formal structure. Some authors suggest that discrimination in the informal structure is even worse than in the formal.[66]

> A very clear example is apartheid in South Africa. Everyone accepted that blacks can be as intelligent as whites, who were the ones in power and limited blacks' access to it. It had to be imposed as an obligation, because whites kept power to themselves and were not about to let another group in. It's a bit like that in companies, there first has to be an obligation in order to create equality. (Manager, 45 years old)

We observed very different opinions when it came to quotas. Whereas men disapproved of them and of consolidated women's networks, women considered mandatory quotas something necessary for their own advance.

2. <u>Men do not recognize a single feminine trait.</u> Feminine is bad. This lack of trust in women harks back to the most ancestral kind of stereotypes and shows up in many comments heard during the group meetings.

> Women have hidden agendas. I worked at a firm where 90 percent of employees were women. The organization chart has nothing to do with the power structure of organizations. As a man, I went in there with a technical job and not too much awareness of what was going on around me. The men spoke clearly, there was some degree of nobility there. Men worked their butts off. But the women will stab you in the back three times, it's dangerous, very dangerous... (Male manager)

> We are evil when we are in power and evil with each other. I have seen very ambitious women who have made it to the top

and then become worse than men. They are the ones who yell at meetings. How sad if that's the only way to make it to director general...But perhaps a male director general would have done the same thing, and wouldn't be criticized for it. (Manager)

What we see here is evidence of Kanter's tokenism theory, in which a woman who exhibits a different behavior leads people to generalize and apply that behavior to the entire minority group. These are organizations that do not accept diversity. It's the queen bee syndrome, the woman who does not help other women when she makes it to the top. Loneliness and a lack of practice may account for excessive anxiety. Both place great limits on upper management.

It's true that when a woman makes it to the top she adopts male patterns. And maybe that means they are mean to the women beneath them. They say women are kind of more jealous. (Manager, 41 years old)

This comment makes explicit reference to management styles, and although there are a few differences, at the training level there are more similarities.

It's very hard to generalize. I have had high-ranking bosses who were men and women. The women seemed tremendously competitive, more so than the men. I don't know why that is. I think women are very demanding on themselves because they feel it is harder to leave their mark. And that is why they can be more brutal than men. Both had very tough characters. (Male manager, 37 years old)

We can see that men admit they don't understand female behavior and are perplexed at the fact that they need to be constantly proving themselves. As for women, many adopt the male model, which turns women into limiting factors for other women. Instead of reflecting on how to change and evolve into a different type of person, what we see is criticism that is far from constructive. There is a criticism of fear, a criticism of lack of training,

behavioral patterns that could be modified if there was a gender awareness and training without falling into the trap of feminist victimism.

> Our firm was on the cover of *Cinco Días* [business newspaper] today and she didn't know about it; she got so mad...She wants to act like a boss so she does the typical male things: doesn't listen, doesn't help, doesn't let you help...she thinks she is more of a boss that way. (Male manager, 43 years old)

> Often we are written off as overly sentimental, accused of wasting time, and I disagree. At the bottom I think there is a bit of fear; men are more accustomed to selling themselves and building alliances with other men, such as a team of four or five men in a company board, where they already know each other's weaknesses, how to walk all over one another or how to lend each other a helping hand. (Manager, 39 years old)

3. <u>Fear of chaos, of no limits.</u> Women ignore the codes imposed by men, their ways, their conduct, which leads them to lose their framework for acting in the workplace. Inasmuch as the rules are not what they used to be, men feel unprotected.

> We are different by nature. I have had a lot of experience with women. I work better with women, they open up new roads...Women behave in such a way that they are on top of everything, whereas I focus on my work and forget everything else. Women perform many tasks at the same time, and that also makes them more vulnerable. She prioritizes, but she must learn how to manage...

This last comment makes reference to a woman's controlling, invasive nature, which is not necessarily exclusive to the female sex. Insufficient information in management occurs almost at all levels of the organizational chart and is not exclusive to either sex or any one type of person.[67]

> I think every company has a corporate culture stating how things are done, and these people have tried to break that mold and

stand out. They want to be noticed so they interfere with what you're doing and how you're doing it.

4. Rivalry and a belief in one's own uselesness because one lacks similar experience to men's, as illustrated by several comments we heard.

Women are fighting for something they believe they don't have, and that's not the way to do things. They make an association out of anything. If you make an association of male managers, you'll see both men and women complain about it. In Madrid the Jockey Club is an all-male club, and that is not logical nowadays, it's very odd. I'm fine with women associating to bring together common interests, like a blondes club for instance.

Women have to understand the company and its needs. But women do not understand this properly. They have to be as ready and up to speed as men. Women have no experience, we managers work from a more empirical base. You buy your own theory. If you go purchase books on upper management written by women, you see they have no experience...

Rather than make regular observations, men display a constant need to undermine, a lack of respect. They have great difficulty viewing women in a transitional process either inside or outside the firm. In the background is a certain amount of envy because of the new rungs that women managers are climbing. But whatever you undermine is no longer desirable, it is neither something to compare with or to compete with.

5. A constant accusation that women are mothers. Their first argument – that women are less dedicated to the firm than men. Very few take up their roles as fathers. The fact that men do not participate in child rearing is no doubt a limiting external factor for women managers. Motherhood is mentioned as an obstacle on the path to upper management. There is also a certain unease at the sexuality lying behind motherhood.

A recently married woman is likely to get pregnant. For the first six years, a woman can ask for a reduced schedule so she can care for the child. It is women managers who are most reluctant to hire other women. I find this hard to understand. (Male manager, 43 years old)

This charge that it is women who have the babies calls upon nature as justification to establish differences. In this sense, speaking of nature is a matter of faith, but also a matter of not questioning the social and organizational changes taking place in a globalized world that are changing people's traditional roles at the social, personal and organizational level.

Touraine, in his recent text "The new social paradigms,"[68] accurately points to the passage from the social to the individual. New roles fit into this context. But let us take a quick look at how men perceive their female colleagues who have positions of authority.

I have had two female bosses and in both cases the relationship was not good. Not because I think they are worth less for being women, but because often a women manager's attitude towards a subordinate man is to establish a distance and make it clear that they're the boss.

The person I worked with here at the Institute screamed a lot. Her leadership consisted of being the one who yelled the most. She didn't listen to reason, and was not open to her colleagues' ideas. When she was in a bad mood there was nothing you could do. She didn't know how to lead.

They try to act the way they think a man would act, although in fact they don't. They try to say: if you think that just because I'm a woman you're going to take me lightly you're wrong. I'm not going to give you any slack because even if I'm a woman, I'm your boss.

I have male friends with female bosses and they have a great relationship with them. I think it's not a question of gender, it's a question of personality. I think it depends on the person, not the sex. Everyone says it's a matter of insecurity.

It is harder for women to make their mark, to have visibility, to be recognized. They want to stand out. They interfere with what you're doing and how you're doing it.

Sometimes they are contradictory. You cannot delegate yet want to do things yourself. She was taking responsibilities away from me, I think in order to stand out more...It's been a common trait of all my female bosses, but it never happened with male bosses – we always established each other's limits...

Establishing distances, yelling, being competitive and contradictory, wishing to act like men, needing to stand out...these are the traits that men see in their female colleagues. There is a culture of undermining female management, which surely creates more pressure for the manager. Interviews showed that after the stage of undermining, there is a period of slight understanding of women's plight, as later statements show. There is also an analysis of the difference between a multinational and a family business, and a consideration of women's role in other societies.

Men and women are different, we have different values and that shows...Women are more intuitive. When you're interviewing someone I always trust a woman's point of view a lot more...they have other abilities.

I don't think it's a question of diversity – you need to have a bit of everything because it's all getting increasingly complex. It's a very simple logic, a different way of looking at things.

It's not the same working for a multinational firm such as this one or for a middle-sized company in Spain. In smaller firms with very local cultural components, women have to fight a lot more because it is still predominantly a man's world.

Another factor to take into account is the nonexistent concept of career versus job. Female managers display fewer work-related ambitions. In terms of unconditional support for the partner, women, save for a few exceptions, are always the ones who are socially and

psychologically predestined to make sacrifices for the other member of the couple.

> Women have to reconcile. Fortunately, my husband has always supported me. Behind every great woman there is always a great man. I had cancer and required treatment. We decided to adopt a child. When we were going through the paperwork I got pregnant…When the child was one year old a project came up in a company with 350 female employees that was on the verge of shutting down. But I had to go to Texas for three months to get up to speed on the case, and when you have a one year-old…But then my husband told me: "If you don't take that job because you think I'm not a good father, I'd be disappointed." So I took it. (Manager, 59 years old)

We tried to understand the male rhetoric regarding changing roles for women managers from the perspective of change in social and organizational structures, exploring the motives behind their statements' manifest and latent violence.

We believe that an economic revolution whose significance may be compared with the industrial revolution is pitting men – especially older men – against younger women who were born in the era of new technologies and who are fluent in their use. The rules of the game have also changed among the members of the company. Now, corporations are virtual entities, they are amorphous, nonhierarchical, and in any case very different from what they used to be. Gender relations have also experienced a significant turnaround. Men born during the demographic explosion were raised to become providers. Halfway through their lives, they find themselves competing with a generation of young professional women with a completely different set of values. All this, without mentioning the social pressure to maintain their youthful looks and perpetual virility. If women do not like to grow old, men are positively scared of it. From a logic of competitiveness there is little space left for reflection. Men, unlike women, rarely talk about the decadence of their virility, and face this transition with greater difficulty than women. According to some authors[69] men are more scared of death, because they are not directly linked with birth and become mere spectators to it. Along the same lines, it is hard for men to accept and understand the changing role

of women. Whereas women need to switch from an emotional logic to a material one in order to cement their independence, men must undergo the inverse process to consolidate and understand equality policies. According to Sheeny,[70] the post-patriarchal man will be able to take on a diversity of roles and to go along with change rather than resist it.

8

The Cinderella Complex Versus Financial Freedom

Financial socialization as a barrier or a springboard

While talking about money is generally considered taboo in many societies, it is even more markedly so when it is women doing the talking. Financial socialization comes from different sources, from the social structure to the family group and also includes culture, corporate culture and the culture of a given career, which might be more or less open to discussing economic issues.

Traditionally it is men who receive the message to produce, whereas women either get the opposite message or are made to understand that their salary will be complementing that of their partner's. Financial behavior seen and heard during childhood becomes a lifelong habit. Often, it is emotional factors such as fear, guilt or greed that ultimately rule attitudes towards money.[71] In the case of women, traditionally they have been socialized to experience the "Cinderella complex,"[72] which Colette Downing defines as a personal psychological dependence consisting of the profound desire for others to take care of us. It is a complex web of long repressed attitudes and fears that have kept women mired in a sort of lethargy and prevents the full use of their faculties and creativity. Just like Cinderella, these women wait for some outside factor to come transform their lives.

On the outside things have changed significantly, though not enough yet. Women have entered the work force on a massive scale, but they have not penetrated upper management. Selfless messages about caring for others and assisting them with their projects, as

well as an education that tends to make women put their own wishes aside, are still common practice. In order to achieve power, if that is really what they want, women must be self-sufficient both at the material and affective levels.

However, when this issue is broached among groups of business women, one still hears sentences such as: "I'm scared," "I have trouble negotiating," or "It's enough for me just to get some recognition." These are routine comments, although not normal ones. These honest statements indicate self-awareness, but if we consider that the entire problem "lies outside," then that becomes the real problem in itself. Younger women especially are becoming aware that some of the problems lie within themselves, in their choices and in the things they give up. We are still coexisting with habits of the past that erode women's self-esteem, as well as educational programs that do not enable them to meet the demands of the current job market. Once we stop making the system, the male gender or family rules responsible, each woman will be able to look deep inside herself and be her own fairy godmother without waiting for a Charming Prince to show up. At the educational level, it's not about what we can do for our children, but "what we should stop doing" so that boys and girls start learning to be self-sufficient. Women must learn to become stronger, while men should not feel guilty about exteriorizing their feelings.

Some of the mandates that women were educated in have lost their worth, especially the ones proclaiming that women should feel protected and fulfilled by a happy married life. Nowadays messages carry other content such as the permission to obtain money and power, and most importantly, the freedom to choose one's partner and decide on the system that works best for each relationship. Slowly, women are perceiving the importance of money as a key variable to obtain personal autonomy. It's no longer about sharing laundry duties, but about sharing power, and this power lies in finance.

The female collective can be a lot stronger if it becomes aware of this fact. Women are discovering, especially in the political arena, how important economic factors are. Ségolène Royal and Hillary Clinton needed vast sums of money to back their campaigns, besides solid arguments against their rivals. Women must show character, integrity, ethical values, clarity and competence, and

must have an educational level in accordance with the positions of upper management that they wish to hold. Women no longer want to be copilots, they want to take the helm of their own lives.

There is no doubt in anyone's mind that we live in a consumer society that often equates possession of material goods and money with power and authority, whereas an absence of the same generates low self-esteem. Domínguez and Robin, in their book "La bolsa o la vida" (Your purse or your life) point out that money is usually a screen on which to develop our lives, a screen on which we project the capacity to make our dreams come true, assuage our fears, mitigate our pain and "make us rise higher." What we feel about money rules our lives far more than any other factor, to which we must add the fact that there is a notorious absence of debate on the issue. Money, together with death and sex, is one of our society's taboos.

We live in a consumer society without precedents. Until relatively not long ago, people were not in a position to purchase as much nor to get into so much debt, nor were there so many references to money in the media. Our parents and grandparents, who lived through world wars, the Spanish Civil War or the 1930s depression, had a very different attitude towards money: they did not like to spend it.

These days, when we buy something on credit, we rarely stop to think about the amount of hours, days and energy we used in order to make that purchase. Not only do we have to return the loan, but pay a high interest on it as well. It is even harder to gauge the psychological cost of being in debt.

We often hear the sentence "time is money," and those in debt must use their time, that is to say their energy, to reduce it. Due to the significance of money in our society, we felt it was important to know what Spaniards felt about it. According to a CIS survey, work, health and family are top among issues that matter most to them, as we can see in the table below. According to it, the greatest source of happiness is "being in good health" (62.3 percent), followed by "enjoying a family of your own" (42.6 percent) and "material security" (33.2 percent).

Men and women differed notably with respect to this last item: men valued it at 38.3 percent, whereas women gave it a 28.8 percent. There is nearly a ten-point difference between the genders. In her research on women's economic dependence, Clara Coria

Table 8.1 Spaniards, Money and Happiness

	Total %	Men %	Women %
Health	62.3	61.2	63.4
Family	47.3	46.2	48.4
Material security, well-being	33.2	38.3	28.4
Being at peace with oneself	26.8	23.3	30.1
Having good relationships	15.6	15.1	16.1
Feeling free	6.4	7.0	5.8

Source: CIS, Study No. 2203

indicates that even if women have a paying job (out of a need or willingness to work), this does not mean that she feels entitled to it.

Table 8.2 underscores how men grant greater importance to material affairs, 55.6 percent versus 51.7 percent. Inversely, women are more afraid of loneliness, rejection or abandonment: 49.2 percent versus 40.9 percent.

With regard to fantasies relating to happiness, what most Spaniards desire is "to travel" at 56.1 percent, followed by "having a good job" at 47.8 percent. There are no major gender differences here, whereas in the "being rich" category men scored 46.2 percent versus a mere 37.8 percent for women.

Another item where strong gender differences can be seen is "having power or influence": 13.1 percent among men versus 6.8 percent among women. These tables show that women afford little mental

Table 8.2 Spaniards and Causes of Unhappiness

	Total %	Men %	Women %
Material insecurity	53.6	55.6	51.7
Loneliness	45.1	40.9	49.2
Loss of values such as friendship	36.2	36.9	35.4
Lack of money	30.4	31.4	29.5
Conditions of modern life	10.2	10.4	9.9
Other	4.8	4.4	5.2
Lack of free time	4.7	5.4	4.0
Lack of interest in work	4.2	4.8	3.6

Source: CIS, Study No. 2203

Table 8.3   Fantasies Linked to Happiness

	Total %	Men %	Women %
Travel	56.1	55.1	57.2
A good job	47.8	47.4	48.3
Being rich	41.9	46.2	37.8
Being intelligent	32.0	29.0	35.0
Being friends with people we admire but don't know	17.5	18.2	17.2
Knowing the future	10.4	14.7	18.0
Living elsewhere	16.3	13.8	18.8
Having great power or influence	10.1	13.1	6.8
Being famous	9.1	9.6	8.6
Traveling to space	8.6	10.9	6.5
Being good-looking and attractive	7.9	7.2	8.6
Having a romance with a star	6.4	7.6	5.2
Being elected to a political post	3.0	4.4	1.7

Source: CIS, Study No. 2203

space to the material dimension. It all leads to a different use of money according to gender: whereas men are taught to use it, women are taught not to.

Money, life cycle and family mandates

The traditional view of money focuses on its being a unique and neutral tool of exchange that merely facilitates monetary transactions. But we are aware that we grant money a lot more value than that, since it becomes the repository of our dreams, fears, wishes, projects and so on. Experience shapes our values, personality, desires, fantasies and fears. Money is present in a person's life from the first moments of development, when the child observes how his parents relate to it (weekly paycheck, economic needs, types of clothing and toys...). Both the child and the teenager observe and analyze, though perhaps not consciously, domestic money games (who brings home the money, who manages it, what each parent spends, gifts, tips,...)

We observed a different financial socialization in our male and female interviewees. Whereas boys in general continue to be told that they must be providers, for women this is still a secondary part

of their training. An additional factor is that many sons experience love and pride from their mothers, whereas daughters not only get less attention, they are also trained to assist others at a very early stage.

> We've all been told by our mothers to "be independent, that will let you make your own decisions." We've all been told to be economically independent. We have been trained to be complementary. I wouldn't mind earning less than my husband, as long as I was making money. Making it to a top position was not among my priorities. (Manager, 53 years old)

We observed the message about the "relative" economic independence, as a complement to a man's wages. These messages can be decoded two ways: "Don't be like me, but don't go beyond certain limits either." Mothers' messages show no indication of ambition or work-related role models; rather, they are messages born of frustration, from mothers' internal glass ceiling. Until relatively recently women worked outside the home only if they needed to, or if their partners did not earn enough to maintain the family, or if they were widowed or divorced, or else the outside world simply regarded it as a whim. The result is that nowadays many women think of their wages in terms of what they need, rather than in terms of its quality and the effort that went into it. In other situations, maternal influence was strong due to the early disappearance of the father figure, in some cases due to death, in others due to divorce. In any case, for whatever the reason, we may assume that the mother took on both roles.

> My mother separated when I was one year old. Now I am 46. I remember her telling me when I was little: "Economic independence gives you political independence," and I have never forgotten that. My mother remarried, and she made a lot more money than my stepfather. She was a manager and she made more, and I have been raised on that. (Manager, 45 years old)

Usually, when it comes to economic affairs, women show a lack of ability to negotiate, by which we mean "all those attempts at trying to reach agreements where there is a divergence of interests and a

disparity of desires." These differences are sometimes unclear depending on whether they occur in the public or private domain, and are more intense in situations where the parts hold a high position. Whereas women are expected to be caring and understanding at the personal level, they are sanctioned if they become competitive at the business level. Younger generations, the ones we described as "competitive," have a different relationship with material things, probably because they were born into a consumer society.

> I work for money. Before I used to believe in fulfillment at work. I would never set up my own business, let someone else give me a paycheck... (Manager, 34 years old)

Many of the interviewees had fathers with very innovative attitudes that encouraged not just independence but also the desire to reach positions of power. The paternal role is developed when the daughters are grown, and their job experience can influence their careers. Interviewed women admitted that their fathers were involved in their career development, appearing as mentors and transmitters of knowledge. According to Burin, male and female subjectivity have more and more things in common, because there are "crossed identifications," the daughter with her father and the son with his mother. Many fathers start developing their paternal role when their daughters are of age. This is the case of many women in our study, who after leaving adolescence behind were strongly encouraged by their parents to develop professionally.[73] Others, however, chose to make twice as much effort as their brothers, spurred by messages encouraging competitiveness.

> My mother had gone to school and was working before she got married. Afterwards she didn't. She encouraged our own training a lot. She didn't buy us brand name clothing but took us to English lessons, guitar lessons, basketball lessons...She clearly wanted to invest in our education, although she also said: "You don't have to be engineers." My brothers, who are all technicians, had a hard time getting their degrees. (Manager, 44 years old)

Often we start from the assumption that women are more conformist, less ambitious, but rarely do we explore the messages

received time and again from society or family that have conditioned "women's mental software."

The sentences we hear are stored away in the attic of our memories, and are only pulled out and dusted during group meetings or coaching sessions, where these forgotten items may see the light of day again. This assumption that women are more conformist stems from the fact that there are confusions (between being selfless or being selfish) which hinder negotiations both at the personal and workplace levels. Faced with this diversity, there are three ways to resolve conflicts: to enforce your will, to yield or to negotiate. According to Coria,[74] it is easy to observe that women would rather **yield** in order to maintain what they call "household harmony," an attitude consisting of avoiding arguments that lead nowhere. Apparently yielding is less violent, but it is only an apparent way of putting a lid on disagreements. According to this author, this is an "appeasement" that is afraid of retaliation by the person we disagree with. This appeasement is very different from strategic yielding, which is a form of temporary renunciation in order to finally achieve the desired goal. Appeasement is a subtle form of submission, which is ultimately the result of multiple invisible violences. What remains unsaid stays lodged somewhere inside our mind, and those uncollectable bills turn into rage, guilt and resentment, symbolized by the disregard for one's own needs.

At the root of this behavior is fear, a feeling that shows up in many group discussions when women are asked what constitutes an inhibitor to their own evolution. Out of fear, many women make unnecessary concessions, tolerate dependencies and silence their opinions, all for the sake of maintaining a so-called harmony.

Out of fear, many women relegate themselves to the sidelines, both in life and in the workplace, until they are ultimately standing outside themselves and their own desires, without always being aware of it. Women are more conformist, that is why they neither fight nor ask for anything.

I have always asked for things, since I was little: I asked my grandfather, my father and a friend of my father's when he was walking down the street. If everyone gets 2, I want 3. Besides that, it was uncomfortable to talk about money at home. If I

asked my father how much he made, my mother told me I was being rude. (Manager, 40 years old)

In European societies, talking about money is synonymous of bad taste, the opposite of North American societies where "time is money." The messages received during childhood condition our relationship to money, as in the case of the earlier interviewee, for whom talking about money at home was considered poor form.

> We were not educated for money. You see women who retire at age 50 or 60 and they say "Look what an insignificant compensation I am getting" and I tell them that now is not the time to complain, if all your life you have put up with 100,000-peseta salaries that's your problem, don't complain now. They complain when there is nothing they can do. (Manager, 46 years old)

Babcock and Laschever[75] estimate that a woman who routinely negotiates her wage raise will earn over a million dollars more when she retires than a woman who simply accepts what she is offered without asking for more. And that is without counting the interest that these extra earnings could yield. We all know that few managers pay more than is strictly necessary. They are prepared to raise the salary if the candidate requests it, but they'll be happy to pay less if they can. Rarely does a boss insist on paying more. A recent study by these authors shows that this is true, even in academia. They talk about a case where professors of similar status but different gender were offered positions as assistants at a US college. After both were hired, the manager realized that the man's salary was significantly higher than the woman's. When he looked into the matter, he was informed that both were offered the same initial salary, but the man negotiated for higher pay while the woman simply accepted the initial offer.

Nobody did anything to fix this difference. The university was saving money and availing itself of the woman's talent and hard work. The manager was unable to see the damage he was doing to his university and to society by not correcting this inequality, and she never knew how much she had sacrificed by not negotiating the offer she was made.

Another example, this time from the negotiating courses at the Kellogg School of Management, was a project to negotiate something in real life. The results showed that those who asked for something for themselves obtained an average revenue increase of 2,500 dollars, whereas those who negotiated in their superiors' name saved some 390,000 dollars. The conclusion reached by both groups was that they were able to negotiate, and that negotiating your first job can mean more than a million dollars' difference when they reach the end of their professional lives. Small initial differences can become great discrepancies with the passage of time.

In another study quoted by the psychologist Virginia Valian in her book Why so slow in the advancement of women, it is clear that there is a notable difference in the "propensity to ask." The study concludes that in general women do not ask, and when they do they ask for less, and usually get less. The final result is a huge disparity in the distribution of resources and opportunities among men and women. In many cases, candidates who pressure to get more pay also get more respect. Women not only sacrifice additional income, they also sacrifice the respect and consideration of their superiors. By having clear ideas from childhood about the importance of money and how to earn it,[76] one can learn commercial skills and financial techniques on how to invest it. If we are not aware of things, then it will be difficult to manage them, much less change them.

> If you are aware, then you can get away. But if you are not, then there is nothing you can do. You have a father who finds you amusing, he does not place conditions on you, but he does limit you...There are people of my generation who support women, very few of them. The man by my side prefers a working woman to a housewife, but he makes you feel like shit because he is always reminding you that you're always talking nonsense. (Manager, 53 years old)

Many women in this situation felt impotence and rage for not having the support of networks[77,78] to revert this situation. The transformation process for this generation was slow and painful, but always constant and self-aware, until the desired results were obtained. Some reached the conclusion that it's better to have

freedom than security, because the latter can atrophy your faculties. Perseverance in the case of women has always been a good ally and a springboard to get ahead.

At first I would systematically cry. I was being disqualified. We had many complexes. My professional development gave me a lot of self-confidence. There came a moment when I developed my self-confidence. Now, at thirty something, I can ask myself "Why is what I'm saying nonsense?" When you can do that, you have managed to overcome yourself. (Manager, 54 years old)

Being aware of one's own low self-esteem – the product of repeated messages that have eroded the self-confidence of women of the transition – is a constant theme in all the statements by women interviewed in this study. But today things are different and they keep changing. The younger woman, whom we call "competitive," makes the same effort as a man, or sometimes even more, in order to get ahead, but she yields a lot less than earlier generations. Still, she feels a significant amount of anxiety over losing her femininity, which translates into a need for approval. We have observed that the women in our study had trouble negotiating. In many cases this was not associated with a lack of intelligence, but rather with symptoms of deeper conflicts linked with gender conditioning.

I am clear about the fact that I want to make money, be it through marketing, wine cellars, real estate or whatever else. I want to make money and if I could retire next year I would – I'd find something to occupy my time. (Manager, 44 years old)

Others have overcome this barrier and feel no qualms about making more than their husbands or partners, while the latter are reaccommodating their roles in favor of the couple's wellbeing.

Sometimes my husband will vomit his frustration on me. If he doesn't like what he's doing, he should do something else. At 40 years old I decided that I was not taking on any more guilt. He is not your average husband…he is an orphan and lived on his own all of his life. His contribution is different. I contribute a lot more money, but he contributes values. We buy property, he

reforms it, and makes more than what he makes in the outside world. But he needs me behind him. When we have worked together things have turned out great. (Manager, 46 years old)

We see there are many ways of managing income, whether as a couple or as a single person. But what is clear is that women who do not ask for more and accept earning less will get just that. Some studies conclude that if women earn more, it's for personal reasons. They are family messages heard and memorized during childhood. It could be that these messages of helplessness have become deep-rooted. Finding out what these messages were can help deactivate them. To these first experiences with material goods we must add cultural and social values. All these make up a structure that affects a person both in her economic and her emotional transactions. If we observe how we use money, we will understand how we act with ourselves and with others. Our interviewees gave us clear indications of this.

Carlos is a 32 year-old man who works for several companies. His colleagues define him as someone who is very dedicated to his job and his people, a very active man. He lives in a small apartment even though his income would allow him to live somewhere bigger. He says of himself that his biggest fault is a tendency to give things away. He is always getting his colleagues little things, as well as his friends, his partner...although he rarely buys things for himself. He gives everything away and keeps nothing for himself.

Carlos is a clear example of emotional poverty. From childhood he has been carrying this loneliness inside, and this affects the way he spends his money: he needs to fill the space around him with people, and he does not think he can do that emotionally, so he brings people gifts, giving them good things in order not to feel alone. He uses money as a way to love others. In short, there are multiple factors that contribute to making people feel inhibited when it comes to negotiating material things.

I have never argued over a salary, I preferred to argue over the schedule. At home I was not educated to make money. I think this has more to do with Christian values than with being a woman. (Manager, 42 years old)

Table 8.4 Financial Socialization and Life Cycle

• Adult experiences with money (work, couple, children)
• Culture, society, religion and money
• Parents and siblings' relationship with money
• Childhood: what parents told them about money

Source: Produced by author

On many occasions we use money like we would affection. We deposit our subconscious desires in it. Once we detect this pattern within ourselves, we can understand that our bank account and our emotional account are not on the same track. Only then can we make more conscious use of our money and focus our desires on more appropriate things.

It is important to differentiate between being independent with our money on one hand and devoted to those we care for on the other. At the subconscious level, there is a deep-rooted social belief that a woman is more feminine the more maternal attributes she possesses. By offering unconditional love, she feels identified with one of the prevailing gender stereotypes. That is why a woman clashes with herself when she defends her personal interest before that of others, or when she can offer a service in exchange for payment. Money implies a conditional exchange with the aim of obtaining a benefit. This is very different from selfless maternal behavior.

The fact that money and affection are not on the same track does not mean they are incompatible. Clara Coria[79] states that a person can have a proper emotional development (tenderness, affection, generosity towards others) yet behave rationally when it comes to money.

Ambition, fear, guilt: values and inhibitions

Another example that illustrates our relationship with money is separation or divorce proceedings. There are many ways a marriage can work, and this will be reflected in the way the divorce is handled. One female executive explained hers:

> Ramón was a control freak and an authoritarian person. I worked as human resources director at a company, and dealt with all the

household chores. Despite that, he would take control over my paycheck and assign me a weekly stipend for expenses. I felt like an irresponsible child when I bought things that were not priority items. Things got progressively worse and I decided to split up. He went crazy. He fought over every item during the divorce proceedings. He did everything in his power to make it difficult and painful for me. (Manager, 42 years old)

Like Susan Forward[80] says, faced with this type of conflict, many women choose to content themselves with a lot less than they would be entitled to. Much the same occurs in the work environment.

I have never asked for a raise. Money was always the last thing; it's work that motivates me, to have fun doing innovative things, not the fact of getting paid at the end of the month. When I came to this company I was not after more money, it was change that motivated me. It's also true that when your basic needs are covered, wages for me were not the main issue. (Manager, 53 years old)

For women, instead of money there is an element of playfulness, "I want to have fun at work, to do innovative things, it's not about getting paid at the end of the month." To have fun working is one of the options, to use money as a weapon is another formula. In the movie "First Wives Club" the main characters say that they are not seeking revenge, because that would put them on an equal footing with their ex-husbands. "What we want is justice," they claim. At one point during the separation process we see a change in paradigm. From feeling jealous over their partner's wealth or power, from seeking revenge, the women realize that they can develop analogous strategies without imitating their exes. When the separation proceedings begin, women, such as those in the movie, realize that the values they thought were theirs because of the authority exercised over them, are not theirs really. They realize that they don't really know what they want, and this is a terrifying moment for them. Support structures break down, marking the beginning of justice and freedom. In fact we have not been educated to feel free to build a new identity. In this sense, money (and the things it can buy) often become the weapon of choice for a spiteful partner as a

way of externalizing his rage when the relationship fails. In short, money is not a mere commercial exchange – rather people project on it emotional issues that are far from obvious. Real prosperity resides in having a lot of what we really want from life, both materially and emotionally.

A woman with low self-esteem settles for getting recognition and being paid less than her male colleagues. Western economies are totally dependent on women's acceptance of lower wages than they deserve. Thus, an ideology that undermines women is imperative in order for them to continue accepting this wage difference as a counterweight to the achievements of the feminist movements.

> I knew I wanted to study engineering because I really like science and felt that by being an engineer I would have access to managing posts. One of my skills is my capacity for organizing. It's good for us women to have degrees, training and so on. I've spoken English since I was little, later I did a master's degree in European communities. We need more support to get to the same place. (Manager, 44 years old)

> Men want power at any cost. We all have professional ambition. They want to be first, to be noticed. Men feel this is enough compensation for not getting along with the others. But we women want everything to be nicer, without tension. (Manager, 42 years old)

Hegelsen[81] clearly describes the behavioral differences between men and women. Male executives have been socialized to compete for the top positions, while women prefer to create an agreeable work environment and stay in middle management. Training is an essential element in career development, besides other items such as the resume and prior experience.[82] Women either are less ambitious, or they are not prepared to achieve things at any cost – we are inclined to think the latter. In other societies as well, it would seem that ambition is not a priority for women; rather, ambition is tailored according to their varying needs at different moments during their life cycle.

> I studied law and started working at the legal department of the Foreign Affairs Ministry in Copenhagen nine years ago. My first

post abroad came a year later in France. Then I returned to Copenhagen and now I work at the embassy. In order to be here I was trained in team management. Our system consists of learning on the job. (Diplomat, 54 years old)

I am very ambitious and I want to do the best job possible. I never wanted to be a leader. If you work at the Foreign Affairs Ministry, the biggest move is to become ambassador. (Diplomat, 54 years old)

According to Barbera,[83] the process of implementing real equality does not only involve gender discrimination in existing legislation or access to training, but it also entails – as observed in Scandinavian countries – promoting processes that get results at a second level, that is to say, moving from equal social status to equal pay. The quota system applied in the more advanced societies were restricted mostly to political circles, and was less successful in business environments.

In Denmark 30 percent of bosses are women, but the figure drops as you reach the upper echelons of the organizational chart. In the last five years there has been a rise. Then there is the matter of reconciling work and family. In Denmark the maternity leave can be shared between the mother and the father, although usually it's the mother who takes it, which always slows down her career a bit. We have very good nursery and elderly care centers, so it's easy to work and have children. But having a high-level career is another matter. (Diplomat, 54 years old)

We can see that a country's culture and work environment can either facilitate or inhibit women's career advancement, but that even in a flexible environment, many women prefer to commit fully to motherhood during the first years of their child's life, even if society makes it easy to share that role.

I didn't think "I'm going to be an executive"; I didn't see myself like the rest of my colleagues. The only ones who achieved management positions were the two of us who were always together.

I had ambition, that's why I went to the United States, because I wanted an international career. (Manager, 41 years old)

Ambition, a desire to get promoted and the resources to achieve it sometimes develop at a very early age without the family necessarily having an influence over it. Other role models, books or promotional campaigns can be the channels that open up women's minds, and show them glimpses of other opportunities.

I've been an entrepreneur all my life. I set up my first business at age ten, providing entertainment for children's parties, and I made a lot of dough. At 16 I set up a clothing store in Argentina. I also studied architecture, although the only thing left from that period is my husband. (Manager, 46 years old)

Another important external factor in female promotion is getting a master's degree. Sometimes because of the high cost and time investment necessary, only one member of the couple gets this type of degree. Still, although master's degrees are a good way to acquire a global vision of organizations and develop a network, they do not guarantee access to upper management positions. And courses in high management are not always met with approval.[84]

My friend, the one who did a master's degree in business administration and management, is now a manager at Endesa. I always had this great drive to achieve things and I was always very active with one thing or another: I went to evening courses, was a volunteer somewhere else...Since I was 14, I have been very active outside the house, that has been a constant theme in my life. (Manager, 45 years old)

According to Mintzberg, management is a practice that blends a good dose of experience with a certain amount of art (perspective) and a bit of science (analysis). We don't need heroes, nor technocrats in positions of influence. We need balanced, dedicated people whose managing style could be described as encouraging.

It is in this 21st century leadership that women's strength resides, since traditionally they have had this leading role in other

Table 8.5   Traits of a Transformational Leadership

Source: Produced by author

environments. It's about trying to liberate this potential developed within her immediate family circle and promoting its use in business groups. The problem lies in the transition from the private to public spheres. In the private sphere, a woman is encouraging of others and helps contain conflict, but in the company she needs to be competitive. These subtle differences are sometimes missed, creating false expectations among the various agents. Being able to extrapolate these motivational skills to the business organization would result in a transformational leadership aimed at freeing up employees' potential in order to maximize their performance at work and let out their creativity and talent.

> I have been a manager since I was 28 and back then I resented being considered too young. I have always sought out my own space. I feel like a manager. I really like to carry out projects and get teams moving. I enjoy the recognition and prestige more than the monetary compensation. (Manager, 42 years old)

When women are asked about their jobs, they say they wish to enjoy their work. This notion came up time and again among the interviewees regardless of age. They also want to transmit this feeling to the rest of the organization. They try to come up with new formulas and optimize people's resources. If we add up

information and emotion, what we get is maximized innovation and creativity, key elements in a society based on knowledge.

> First of all comes innovation and creativity, to question yourself and find new ways of doing things. Second comes creating teams and knowing how to manage people's potential. You have to create your little orchestra where you have everything you need. I am a team woman. And third, you need to have the ability to analyze and synthesize. Because I have that inner freedom, I cross the boundaries set by organizations. I think we women mobilize companies more. I am a network creator: I keep up contacts and relationships. (Manager, 59 years old)

Women prioritize team work not just because it is something they have been developing at the family level, but because it is one of the possible organizational formulas in this new capitalism that has been so well described by Sennett.[85] One of this author's key questions is asking how a society with short-term views can be asked to pursue long-term goals. This is a society that instills fear into its citizens: fear of losing their jobs, fear of losing control over their lives, fear of not being able to reconcile work and family and seeing their children turn into consumer rats at shopping malls. This fear, for many women, is combined with a low self-esteem which in turn results in low gender solidarity. This is why team work and networks are a way of consolidating bonds in a society that stands out for the weakness of its bonds. Team work consists of moving from one task to another and evolving during that process. Solid links depend on sustained interaction.

> Men also build teams, but they are different, there is a different managing style. The authoritative manager who always gets a "yes, bwana" is no longer going to triumph. Women manage through consensus and persuasion. They do not manage through loyalty, but through merit. They manage teams who produce new ideas. Women always train a successor because they know that if they are not there one day, somebody has to replace them. (Manager, 59 years old)

The fact that women can give birth and experience that space between life and death makes them better able to ponder the end of

Table 8.6   Production Eras and Work Relations

• Wisdom era
• Knowledge worker
• Information era
• Industrial era
• Agricultural era
• Hunter-gatherer era

their professional mandate or even their lives. Because men cannot experience procreation first-hand, it is harder for them to think about death or about the end of a period.

Whereas both men and women manage teams, women try to create a permanence in time, even if all it means is finding a successor – in an underlying manner she is betting on continuity and the consolidation of bonds. We observe that management models have evolved according to the changes occurring in production forms and models. The female management style, based on abilities, is more in tune with today's society. We assume that this is the era of the knowledge worker and that by wisely integrating head and heart we can achieve better results.

> Some women do not wish to reach the top. For half of women, work is not the main thing. I would rather read, go to a concert or watch a movie. Women do not stick around just so the boss will see them. In Germany for instance, nobody stays at work longer than 5pm, and if you do it means you are a bad, unproductive worker. (Manager, 53 years old)

Managing styles in some of the firms we consulted are still of the controlling variety: control over schedules, which makes employees spend hours glued to a chair; in short, old-fashioned models that are in disagreement with the skills and responsibilities of the knowledge worker. Authority creates respect but authoritarianism and control create a significant rejection. That is why Juan José Almagro, in his book,[86] points out that people leave their bosses, not their companies. Women try, although they do not always succeed, to develop a new management style that is more attuned to current trends, away

from the controlling styles that stunt the development of people's potential.

> Men today are educated differently, and run things like women. There are not so many women because they have entered the job market at a later date. Spain is one of the European countries with the lowest birth rate. It's not looked upon favorably at work if a woman gets pregnant, whereas in northern countries this matter has been resolved. If you look at a woman's career, she misses work less than a man. (Manager, 59 years old)

Sennett[87] also points to the conflict created by trying to reconcile work and family, especially the uneasiness of having to neglect the children's needs because they do not fit into the pattern of work demands. Commitment to a company is not usually "long-term," but commitment to one's children is. Not being able to reconcile such different spheres brings trouble to both fronts.

> In order to reconcile both worlds, first schedules need to change. I would only say one thing about it: daycare centers, daycare centers, daycare centers. And extracurricular activities at school until 7 or 8 in the evening. When we have that, women will be ready to accept executive responsibilities. For some women it's not that they don't want them, it's that they simply cannot accept them. (Manager, 50 years old)

We see how ambition can influence possibilities for promotion. Apparently, women are less ambitious than men. We think this is not the case, but that their principles make them prioritize other aspects at different stages of their lives. They reduce their ambition in order to reconcile. In the political arena, women no longer beg for crumbs, but have climbed onto the power wagon without waiting to be rescued or recognized. Women need to understand their recent past and push aside obstacles and barriers. An image change is needed to move forward in an "elegant and intelligent" manner, leaving behind the fear of returning to a situation of apathy.

> Women are just as ambitious as men, but they are not as aggressive. You can be ambitious but in a peaceful way, by negotiating.

Men are colder and more aggressive. They don't mind stepping all over other people as much. There are also nonaggressive men who act just like women. But I have met more aggressive and ambitious men than aggressive and ambitious women. (Manager, 59 years old)

In short, we see how low self-esteem and renunciation are big barriers to reaching upper management positions. On the contrary, having networks and mentors facilitates access to the top. We could almost say there is a transition: before, women passed from their father's hands into their husband's; now it's from the father's into the mentor's. A good bond and paternal encouragement are the basis for seeking similar bonds at work. Among interviewed women we noticed a certain degree of difficulty developing female networks. Often it is women who are harshest on their peers, as a result of their own low self-esteem. Besides being capable of developing networks and inner teams, the external network is more difficult to create because it means investing an additional amount of time that women do not have.

At the management level things work at a man's pace. Important meetings are scheduled for 7pm. Men go have lunch and develop their networks. They solve things socially, whereas women are sitting at their desks doing the work. (Manager, 40 years old)

That happens at advertising and communications firms. There are no women at the top but you move down and it's all women. Upper managers are nearly always men. They help each other out; it's all about networks. (Manager, 42 years old)

The extra available time is used to solve domestic or family problems, whereas men, given their more one-dimensional character, have extra time to relate to each other or share hobbies and leisure time. As for the mentors, it is easier to give a promotion to someone you identify with and is part of your inner circle.[88]

I always had a mentor or someone who supported me. I am an educator. I went to the United States to specialize in education and a professor there helped me to stay for three years. When I returned, another man asked me if I would be codirector with him. I was with

him for seven years. At this last post it was a male colleague who recommended me. I owe my entire career development to the support of men, especially my father. (Manager, 42 years old)

For women, the network is the extension of a previous web created by the support of the father figure. But in any case, the strength of networks lies in the weakness of bonds of commitment within an organization.

I have seen that men know how to create their own networks. They have their little clique and I am left out of it. It simply does not occur to them. They have their own codes, which I don't know. It is a very subtle thing and they don't mean anything by it. I know they value my work highly, but I am just not part of the clan... (Manager, 43 years old)

These are closed power circles that feed on informal contacts, golf games, soccer matches and other leisure activities. Many commercial deals are closed at such moments. Women, on the contrary, give priority to affection and personal development.

Men are used to having their clans and their different codes. A very curious thing I see every day is that secretaries call the men "Mr" while they call me "you." They don't mean anything by it. But I think women have a hard time helping other women maintain their position. (Manager, 40 years old)

There is a constant theme among women: if they detect a different attitude towards them, even from their own employees, they tend to find excuses for it. "They don't mean anything by it," it's a smoke screen, blindness to a gender stereotype. It's as if there were different fenced territories, one for men and networks and money, another for women and selflessness and nurturing. Behavior changes with age, social class, family specialization and self-esteem. We observe the degree of emotion that predominates at different moments and during decision-making processes.

I had a boss who was communications director and he taught me the ropes. Later, the director general of my company trusted me

> blindly. He was a very open, tolerant person with a high self-esteem. The worst thing that can happen to you is to find an insecure person above you, who keeps blocking you. He trusted me at first and then gradually gave me more responsibilities. (Manager, 44 years old)

It is a given that a top executive will have a high IQ. Higher education and international master's degrees attest to this. But emotional intelligence is a much more subtle thing that allows one to detect through intuition things that escape reason. In our era of flexibility, this represents a highly sought-after quality, as long as there is an awareness and a control of emotion, not a emotional overflow, which would represent a basic assumption type. It's not a question of gender, but of emotional maturity and trust in one's own abilities.

> My approach to the company is absolutely emotional. I truly believe that emotions move the world, that is to say, the left side of the brain, the rational part, is completely subordinated to the emotional side...I like working with women, they are more transparent, more assertive. We get along better with women clients, and there are more women clients in managing positions. (Manager, 46 years old)

The first skill that comes with emotional intelligence is being able to detect one's own emotions in order to be able to empathize with others. On the other hand, women have been socialized to show their emotions, while men were raised not to.

> Women are not afraid to get in touch with their own weaknesses, but men are...I told myself "In this company you're going to have to be tremendously political, you're going to have to fight for your space." Sometimes my children and I have reflection sessions and I ask them if they would have preferred a different type of mother. It's true they ask me for more time, but if I hadn't done what I like, what would I have brought home? Probably frustration, frayed nerves... (Manager, 42 years old)

As time passes, roles and contents are leveling out. Men who felt trapped in their almost exclusive roles of providers are trying to dis-

cover other sides of their personality ruled by emotion. This is the post-patriarchal man.

> I think that men also have their feminine side. At certain times, men are colder than women while women take the firm as something more personal. A woman thinks she is being attacked, while a man can keep enough distance to say "They are not attacking my work but my authority"...women are no less ambitious, they are less aggressive. (Manager, 59 years old)

Women do not need to maintain a distance so much as men, and they are not afraid to praise the work of their employees. They usually do not feel the need to show off their authority. All this means that women can maximize their subordinates' potential.

> If you have a team of women under you, you take good care of them. I think that's because we are insecure and have a hard time believing we deserve to be where we are. (Manager, 42 years old)

In group discussions and interviews, the issue of insecurity came up openly, yet "one doesn't talk about these things." The moment one is authorized to look at fears and insecurities in the face, these are automatically minimized. When women realize that their peers are feeling the same way, they relax and feel understood. They start to become aware that they don't need to be proving things all the time, or work twice as hard. When they relax that self-demand they can act more assertively. But behind the fear stands freedom, and that is scary at first. Freedom offers a wide range of opportunities, but it also entails new demands, such as growing alone without the support of someone stronger or making one's own decisions without the protection of a father, partner or mentor. When these barriers are overcome, a woman can lean back on her own sense of security and convey this self-confidence to her peers.

> When I went into banking there were very few women. I gave promotions to 24 of them. These days, out of 12 director generals, four are women. Many women are entering academia, although there are few who hold chairs. At US symphony orchestras there was only 10 percent female representation, they said

that women could not conduct...until someone in Boston said "All right, let's act like we're blind when we do auditions, and only listen to the music" and that's when women started to enter the field. (Manager, 47 years old)

Self-confidence and a high self-esteem confer the authority to take and to delegate. The opposite creates a sense of guilt, like a group discussion noted: "I have to say I'm sorry for being successful." This feeling is clear in the following comment – feelings of guilt when one transgresses socially expected roles or ignores gender stereotypes.

Today I read something that said that because we women feel guilty, we always end up with the burnt piece of toast. At work I try to do everything perfectly and I take on whatever it takes. (Manager, 42 years old)

The question remains, why do women feel guilty if things go well (fear of success) and tend to take the burnt piece of toast? Because of an early socialization that has to do with dependence, women (at least the "integrated" ones in our group) feel the need for someone's support. Objectively, many women are aware that they were not raised to recognize and fight for their own desires and for their rights, because otherwise there would be no disparity between their achievements and their desires. As for men, it is not nature that gives them their self-confidence, but their training. They have received lessons in independence ever since they were little. They have not been socialized to express their emotions or to spend time with their young children. These are roles that they were not educated to fulfill, thus their difficulty to take them on.

Thank God we women are taught something that men, and also some women, must learn: that crying is not a sign of weakness but an escape valve and a way to prevent getting liver cancer. Women are less moderate in their emotions and link their phobias and preferences more when they interact with other people. (Manager, 37 years old)

Men have different priorities. First they gauge whether a group is going to help them reach their goal, and later they see whether

there is a good working climate. For that, a man focuses only on the president, the CEO, the man who makes the decisions. (Manager, 44 years old)

Men start off with a plan and clear goals and create their strategy based on that, while women say:

Intuitively we have other priorities that escape them. They really trust me, and sometimes I don't even need to provide explanations. The business world is a very reasoned world. Managers are often engineers and they rely a lot on data. I trust intuition more. We are less trained in argumentative speech and looking at things through figures. In my case they really value that other side. I am surrounded by men who, although they are very finance-oriented, can appreciate that complementary component. (Manager, 41 years old)

We are entering a new era where rigid categories are beginning to blur and there is an attempt at identifying the issues that need to be encouraged in each gender. Men have been traditionally socialized in the need to produce. The man who provided for his family has long been the rule, and men were not trained to provide emotional nourishment for their children, display affection or share the responsibilities of rearing them. Because they had nobody to learn from, they cannot be condemned for not knowing how. On the other hand, women have been constantly raised in the role of motherhood, beginning with games and moving on to other realities. Women have not learned the skills to be effective and develop a career plan.

I think there is a very good thing now, which is that men can work on their feminine side. Today's man is allowed to be a father and to act like one. I think this will bring very good things, more balance, another model based on people. We can both develop both areas, but we need to readjust. Before, men were there and women were here, and now in order to be more flexible we need to break with all the previous patterns and try on new roles. And that cannot be done from one day to the next. (Manager, 41 years old)

What we effectively observe is a confusion that permeates the entire study, which stems from the fact that both men and women are in a

crisis situation because they have lost their references, since most of what they learned within their family circles does not apply to the requirements of today's society. We are currently in a transitional period, trying to find a new balance and a readjustment of roles. This new freedom must result in new workplace identities that enable us to function in the era of the knowledge-based society without the need to give up important aspects of life such as paternity, maternity or economic autonomy for both genders.

9
Conclusion

The main goal of this study was to explore the internal and external causes that limit or encourage women in their transition to upper management positions. This broader goal had several secondary goals aimed at gaining a deeper insight into the structural, organizational and personal factors that condition this situation. In order to clear up each of these levels of analysis, let us go over a few basic concepts used throughout the study.

General concepts and basic concepts

What is meant by upper management?

An upper manager is someone who, in turbulent environments, can have a positive influence on his/her colleagues in order to achieve superior results in a given situation. The manager must encourage personal development so people can grow personally and professionally. Besides maximizing profits, the manager tries to give every employee a voice of his/her own. We consider that upper management is a space where top-level decisions are made and strategies implemented.

Characteristics of the modern company

In general terms, the conditioning factors of global society are radically different from those of earlier eras, when corporations could contain, not create anxiety, as they do at present. When we talk about a "containment environment" we are talking about creating a safe space that helps people face conflict and anxiety. On the other hand, competition for the top positions is getting extreme. This is fueled by certain higher education programs (MBAs) that take this rivalry to its limits, favoring egocentric personalities that represent the opposite of teamwork. Some business schools produce managers who are "blind to emotions," a bit like color-blind people. This blindness may be reinforced by companies that reward "the aggressive loner," who is more often found among the ranks of executive men than women.

At the same time, we are seeing a rise in violent behavior at all levels, with the containment medium replaced with an anxiety-creating environment. There is a risk that is much more relevant than time, which is losing our sense of humanity, of being a person, and becoming confused about which bonds really matter.

Hypervelocity

We feel that due to the influence that hypervelocity has on people's activity, it is important to explore this concept in greater detail. Jeremy Rifkin[89] underscores that nowadays everyone wants to join the information era and to be connected. However, the information and telecommunications revolution is speeding up human activity at such a pace that it can harm people.

Experiments at Harvard and Princeton Universities suggest that we are embarking on a era where "life is organized at the speed of light," that is to say, at 30,000 km per second. Each day we see new computer programs that compress time and accelerate activity, so that we may live in "the age of the second." A few years ago we thought that technology would give us more time to do things. But now we find ourselves asking the uncomfortable question of whether this technology is not turning us increasingly into slaves, cornering us into a dead end. A new term, "24/7," is beginning to define new parameters of time frontiers. Nowadays we have the feeling that we have less time for ourselves than any other people in

the entire history of humankind. E-mail is very useful but we find ourselves answering messages for the better part of the day. Similarly, the cell phone saves a lot of time, but it makes us permanently available for anything that requires our attention. We are immersed in a much more complex and interdependent world than before. Each passing minute is an opportunity to create another link. Descartes' famous "I think, therefore I am" is being replaced with "I am connected, therefore I am." The signs of anxiety over the issue of time are everywhere to be seen. More and more people feel exhausted because of the information overload and because they simply cannot keep up with the pace.

Workers' loss of identity

Job discontinuity, company relocation (taking the headquarters to other countries where labor is cheaper) and mergers and acquisitions[90] generally limit the creation of a workplace identity.

The latter requires, first of all, some continuity at the workplace in order to establish links[91] (understood as the need to create deep emotional bonds), which in turn creates a sense of security.

Sennett[92] and Bauman[93] agree that what society extracts from individuals is their identity. Confusion over identity is present both in men and women, who have had to reposition themselves to adapt to the new work requirements of global society.

These authors place the notion of organization within the broader system of flexible capitalism, which takes workers from permanence at a post to an employment discontinuity that hinders the construction of a basic trust born out of bonds between people. In this networked society, the most salient feature is the power of weak bonds as opposed to the strong bonds that develop over time.

In turn, flexibility determines that people have more time to shape their own lives. Before, individuals had the chance to build an identity at work through cooperation with others. It was more commonplace to receive and project emotions, as well as to solicit feedback on progress at work. Nowadays, employment discontinuity and virtual teams prevail.[94] Fear is a central emotion and an important part of working life. Conflict arises from the loss of control of one's own time due to a growing hypervelocity and an employment discontinuity that also escapes the worker's control. "Policies for reconciling" are only the tip of the iceberg of a much more complex

social problem. The underlying fear is that children may get trapped in an "exaggerated consumerism" while the parents are working and unable to care for them directly. Bureaucracies are exchanged for "networks." The increase in short-term job commitment hinders the creation of solid bonds between people. Nowadays, what is taken from the worker is not added value but his identity.

The female perspective

Life cycles

The life cycle has not been excessively analyzed in the social sciences literature. Sigmund Freud explored the development of personality, especially during childhood, and its later influence on adult life. Carl Jung focused more on middle age and the conditioning factors of the social context. Erik Erikson adopted an intermediate position between both. Levinson[95] and Sheehy[96] analyzed the traits of men's lives. Kets de Vries[97] explored job and personal satisfaction at various stages in the life cycle.

Depending on the age groups, we found it relevant to divide them into three different stages: the first years of confrontation with reality, a second period of consolidation, and a third stage corresponding with mid-life crisis. This concept is very useful to understand the various expectations of men and women at the workplace.

We also created two groups of women that we called "competitive or fragmented" (30 to 45 years old) and "integrated" (46 to 60 years old). Both groups fall back on a characteristic that was described by the founding fathers of sociology, from Simmel to Le Play,[98] who pointed out that "a woman is the basic tool for keeping order, but not for safeguarding her own interests but those of others," to Carol Gilligan and Clara Coria, who underscore women's tendency to "live according to others" and their trouble creating a project of their own.

The youngest ones have before them a well-beaten path, an open labor market, but evidenced a greater personal confusion. They are highly competitive but this collides with their need for approval. There is scant gender solidarity. They see their working life as a yes-no proposition, never do they contemplate integrating both dimensions, which basically means renouncing family life. They have few role models and are under great pressure from the beauty

myth. They try to do everything and feel very guilty if they cannot manage. Only a few of them prioritize. Motherhood is no longer a priority for this group. The life cycle crisis is experienced at around 30, when they start thinking about it. If they get trapped by their careers, they run the risk of missing out on their own lives.

For the older women, the integrated ones, the main problem was finding themselves in a hostile social environment that frowned upon their desire for change. They had no doubts as to maternity. There is a strong gender solidarity among them. They had a lot of trouble reconciling work and family, but they knew they were not ready to give up having children. We were able to ratify that women show a greater need for work and family reconciliation, which in turn creates a greater tendency to feel frustration and accept giving things up (symbolized, on occasion, by a greater tendency to depression). This generation was socialized in the "ball metaphor," meaning prioritizing other people's games instead of one's own.

Family socialization and emulation of role models

We believe that family socialization and role models at home are an important conditioning factor in career evolution. Explanations focusing on internal barriers are associated with gender socialization, which hinders professional success.

We verified a trend formulated in our third hypothesis, which is that women are not less "ambitious" than men, but rather that they put personal issues ahead of professional ones, and this occasionally limits their career aspirations.

References to the past or to female role models that worked for their mothers are no longer valid, and the male work identity model clearly is of no use to them. They find themselves facing the need to build their own workplace gender-oriented identity in order to get ahead. There are crossed identifications, given that the fathers often serve as models and mentors.

The father's influence is a basic element that guides the professional choices, strategy and evolution of women. The fathers were socialized in the role of providers and in that sense they are especially well-placed to help their daughters with their career choices, evolution and ambition. We detected the vital importance of family messages, especially paternal ones, in the case of women – either to assist or inhibit their career development.

The mother figure is decisive in the social construction of identity. For most of the interviewees, the main message was for them to be economically self-sufficient, but not necessarily ambitious. There is a constant theme in mothers, which is a differential, positive treatment of male children, an attitude that subconsciously creates strong feelings of rivalry that will create the basis for competitiveness.

There is scant financial socialization among women. This constitutes an inhibiting factor in salary negotiations, because we have the paradox that if they don't ask for more, they will not get it, whereas their male colleagues insist on this aspect first of all.

There has been a socialization in multiple roles in the private sphere. The matter becomes more complex when these skills need to be taken to the workplace. The multiplicity of roles that need to be played can generate a sense of feeling overwhelmed, as well as a certain amount of authoritarianism at home. This behavior, when taken to the workplace, is counterproductive and makes subordinates use gender stereotypes, such as calling this woman "hysterical." This attitude is not due to any incapacity on her part, but rather to an emotional overflow that pushes her to administer "the power," something that she is still unused to. For this type of woman, authoritarianism works as a façade, a sort of armour built to hide her fear, her guilt, her insecurity or her extreme exhaustion.

Women have a double problem because at home they have to provide emotional nourishment and hold up the family, while at work they must be competitive like everyone else.

Sometimes women find themselves trapped between the old social clichés and radically new ideas. Between wanting to provide entirely for themselves and wanting to have someone there for support and to raise children with. These disparate feelings create a chronic ambivalence that wears women out.

A lot of the observed behavior derives from external barriers that are the result of a patriarchal culture that creates asymmetric relationships between men and women. It would seem that some notions formulated by the forefathers of sociology still prevail, such as Georg Simmel's idea that the only existing culture is the male culture, and his call for an independent female counterculture. Of all the classics, it is Simmel who devoted more time to the female condition and feminist movements, making a difference between the idealized model of "a woman's being" and what she "must be."

Emile Durkheim, on the contrary, defined women as evolutionary fossils, and did not place them within a socio-cultural sphere but in nature. Marianne Weber talked about "the ice-cold hand of reason" and the need to make marriage "an egalitarian space in the union of souls." Lastly, Talcott Parsons, who represents conservatism at all levels, including women, said that men have "the instrumental role" and women "the expressive role." Alberdi[99] pointed out that for Parsons, the man takes care of the economic aspect while the woman's role is to stay at home and socialize the children. In short, while the man is the material provider, the woman takes care of emotional management.

Access to the job market

We are missing a mental representation of the demands made on women at various stages of their lives, which creates a certain confusion that is made manifest at the time of being hired, when they are asked whether they are married and/or pregnant. In the first place, this question intrudes upon the private sphere and is not necessarily linked to the capacity required of the job. If a differentiation cannot be established between the personal and professional worlds, both by the employer and the employee, this will necessarily lead to confusion. What's more, women will be penalized for their reproductive capacity.

Furthermore, companies' rejection of women of a reproductive age hinders career development and becomes an important limiting factor. Companies do not value the emotional abilities that come with motherhood, such as the possibility to encourage people's development and the ability to contain anxiety at times of great competitiveness.

We observed that, for women at the top, a great deal of their success is due to the existence of male mentors who helped them get promoted, whereas there are fewer top-placed women who acted as mentors for other women. Some female executives acted as "queen bees," hindering others from rising to the same spot. Access to networks and training is more limited for women because they have less time than men to indulge in afterwork activities.

We also observed that during the selection process, companies will choose a man over a woman because they assume that he will be more faithful to the firm and not miss work due to parenting issues.

Men display greater competitiveness and thirst for power, which does not necessarily guarantee loyalty to the company if they receive more interesting offers elsewhere.

Basic and graduate training

When it comes to basic training, there are fewer women than men who take up technical careers such as engineering, although in others such as architecture the number of female students is growing exponentially. As for grades, women generally do better than men. One of the basic requirements to access top positions and develop a network is to have a master's degree from a business school. The presence of potential female executives at these schools is generally very low. This scant representation may be due to things such as the high cost of the studies, or an incompatibility of schedules, or the aggressive and competitive style that develops at these schools.[100]

Another important element that hinders promotion at the workplace is a lack of training in management skills (negotiation, decision-making, time management, use of one's own power and strategizing), especially when it comes to developing a plan for one's own career rather than just executing a series of jobs.

We observed a shortage of coaching programs for women managers. Their problems are different from men's, and some of them need assistance with issues such as the balance between altruism and selfishness or reconciling motherhood with work, without falling into a sense of guilt for abandoning their children. On the other hand, firms invest less money on these women-oriented programs because they are considered less profitable.

Education or giving up on a partner and a family

Social pressure affects more intensely those women who are considered (from a predominantly male culture) unfit to rise to the top because of the likelihood of their having children. This is considered a "woman's problem." In reality, it is a social problem that must be resolved at the social level and at the company level, including maternity leave as part of the working contract.

There is a belief in "eternal motherhood" without discriminating between initial periods that demand great dedication from women and later periods where the mother's presence does not need to be so intense anymore.

On one hand they want to be mothers, on the other they do not wish to give up their career advancement, a position that is legitimate given the significant investment they made in their own education. Among the younger women, it is possible to define types. The first type embraces a conscious renunciation of a partner and/or motherhood. Men do not seem to be aware of this new place occupied by motherhood. Although women have unconsciously reduced their own functions, men are still not ready to take over, a fact that is obvious in the scant paternity leaves that are taken – the reason being that men feel this could throw their masculinity into question. There are other women who have stable partners but decide not to have children. A third group is comprised of women who have children and postpone their professional ambitions. A fourth group is made up of late mothers[101] who are living postponed lives. Lastly, a minority of women move their need for affection onto other members of the family: nieces and nephews, elderly parents, or even to nonprofit groups; sometimes they accept postings to developing countries.

• *The couple:*

Among younger women in particular, we observed question marks regarding which of the two needs to change models. It would seem that "men are searching for a woman that no longer exists, while women are searching for a man that does not exist yet." The ideal would be a model that allows both of them to grow emotionally and professionally, that is to say, a model that allows for reconciliation. When there is coresponsibility, as some of the interviewees said, then integration is possible. Younger generations show changes in their attitude to commitment and its benefits. It is the post-patriarchal era. This era creates greater access to emotional development, which until now was off limits to men. This is also positive for children, because they have two references present in their lives from an early age.

Another option is to either accept the game or break up the couple. Accepting can mean abandoning one's career temporarily or even permanently to raise the children, leaving professional development aside. This would be the traditional option of "living for others" or the so-called "ball metaphor," which parks one's own game by the kerb. Another option, which is even more drastic, is to break up with one's partner in order to avoid these dilemmas altogether.

· *Motherhood:*

This is the great dilemma of many of our younger interviewees, who still identify with prevailing stereotypes but do not know whether to view motherhood as a stage or as a lifetime calling. They are trapped in this dilemma for a period of time, identifying with the identity model given by their biological dimension, not thinking about the difference between sex (the biological difference) and gender (the cultural difference). This confusion creates problems when it comes to making a decision, especially when they are accessing the work force.

In a concomitant way, there are other issues such as whether motherhood is compatible or incompatible with career advancement. Interviewees, especially the integrated women, resolved the matter in different ways. Some chose to keep working the entire time, albeit reducing their aspirations. We did not observe that partners took turns when it came to solving a problem; it was a given that women had to deal with it alone. Some hold that it is possible to work and pay attention to your family, but it is necessary to prioritize at different stages. One cannot expect, as some interviewees said, to be the best professional and maintain the same level of dedication to the family. This was the behavior among the integrated women, who often appeared torn. Today's generation tends more towards a renunciation of motherhood, thus cutting away an important part of their personalities.

A third group asks itself how long they should postpone motherhood for the sake of their career. These are the late mothers, who sometimes end up adopting children. Those who opted for these postponed lives experience its advantages and inconveniences. Among the former, the chance to consolidate their careers; among the second, the lower energy levels at the time of having their first child. Spanish society, until now, compared with other European countries, has not been particularly helpful to pregnant women. Scandinavian countries and Germany, for instance, have much more advanced reconciliation policies.

After motherhood

Some women whose children are grown up and have left the home ask themselves, at the end of this period, how to get back in touch

with their own desires, their own projects, especially with more of a time constraint ahead of them. Some are aware of this liberation, once their children have been raised and their parents taken care of, but they ask themselves whether it is not too late in the game to be recovering their freedom. These are painful questions for women who have given up everything, their own lives, for the sake of others. Older women in some cases have acted as springboards for their husbands, and when the husbands got there they began a new life with a younger woman who was less worn out by so much effort.

Another decision facing these women is whether to embrace what's left of life alone or with a partner (the same one or a new one). Both younger women and older ones had the chance to express their feelings regarding this loneliness, as well as the difficulties of getting ahead with little social or family support. Women, unlike men, enter the emotional terrain very quickly in their struggles, difficulties and problems with their children. They find in their peers a support and an understanding that is not there at the social level.

Among the integrated group, we see a belief that the greater the professional success, the worse the emotional life. But younger women accept more naturally the role inversion of men with lower salaries or different schedules who may be civil servants and have time to deal with household chores. Others prefer solitude and put their jobs ahead of everything else so as to not interfere with their career advancement.

Women at the workplace

The first thing we noticed were the extremely high demands placed by women on themselves. It would seem that they have to work twice as hard as men, that they have to prove themselves in order to achieve recognition. Possibly for this same reason, women need to place limits on others and on themselves. Men want to work from an early date, whereas women postpone the beginning of their careers. Women have better grades, but less practice in the labor market. We noticed that these self-imposed demands lead women to a level of exhaustion that sometimes ends in anxiety attacks. It is important to keep in mind that women participate as much as or more than men in their own "devaluation."

Women as subordinates

The search for mentors.   The study found that many men have helped women rise within a company by acting as mentors, as have many fathers who helped their daughters grow professionally by instilling in them a sense of ambition and a work ethic. Interviewees of all ages admitted to their fathers' influence in their career development. Some, however, had fathers for whom their daughters were an amusement, or worse yet, who were ashamed of having a female child. We observed significant discrimination within families when it came to the treatment received by the male children, especially from their mothers.

Critical admiration.   There was a clear admiration for the father figure. As the boss, the man is usually proactive in his professional activity, which generates admiration and imitation in women. There is scant gender solidarity, with women often being very negative and critical of each other. This scant gender solidarity is greater when self-esteem is lower. Women display greater difficulty in maintaining their authority in upper management positions.

Competitive or collaborative women.   These women are highly competitive. When they work with other women there is a lot of tension because they do not accept each other's authority. Some women in upper management positions say that while their secretaries address men as their superiors, they themselves are addressed by their first names. Work relations are often very different when it's men working with men, when it's women working with women, or when there is a combination of the two. There is a different communication style and decision-making process. Women feel more guilty/responsible if things do not work out the way they were supposed to. They are subjected to a "social Darwinism" represented by the beauty myth. Since women have become materially stronger, they need to be mentally weakened so they will not reach positions of real power. In men's eyes, the more attractive ones are seen as sexual objects, making the beauty myth a factor for promotion or discrimination within the firm.

Women display a constant need for approval. They need for everything to be harmonious, and above all they want everybody to love them. They complain about accepting the most unrewarding tasks,

but sometimes they lean the ladder against the wrong wall. They are afraid of criticism but are extremely critical with themselves.

Unlimited availability? When it comes to availability, they are less ready to live only in relation to the company, especially if they wish to reconcile work with a family life. This makes them place limits on their own ambitions and reconsider their position. They make sacrifices without expecting gratitude. If they opt for unlimited availability, then they are giving up on other areas of life.

Women as equals

How to defend their interests. We observed that women have a hard time defending their interests. They ask for little and are insufficiently trained in negotiating skills. They have trouble evaluating their own work in material terms, and always need to be proving something. They give themselves no respite.

Ambition and its limits. What is the price that must be paid to keep rising? What costs are acceptable and which unacceptable when trying to reach upper management positions? We observed great ambition among the younger women, those who want to reach the top. They want to be good friends, executives, competitive, good-looking. They embody the ideal of 24/7 dedication, that is to say, being active 24 hours a day, seven days a week. This ambition enslaves them in the name of an ideal that they can hardly hope to reach, in addition to their low tolerance for frustration. They are trapped in the age of hypervelocity. Dispersal and a difficulty to prioritize makes them weak. They feel guilty if they take a break.

Women as superiors

The new female manager is full of contradictions. She can enforce her will, but often she feels bad about it. She also knows that she is being observed (token theory, Rosabeth Moss Kanter) because she is part of a minority group whose actions are carefully monitored and extrapolated to the rest of the female community.

When working with people, they incorporate affection into their management style: women perceive that motherhood gives them skills that make them different from their male colleagues. They have

moved from the selfishness of thinking only about themselves to thinking about others and their needs. This attitude, taken to the workplace, gives them a great advantage. These women are like symphony conductors who can extract the most out of each musician. They know how to listen and provide encouragement at times of weakness. Their search for harmony makes them create healthier work environments. They know how to get close to people.

They need to fend off clichés and build new models, to be "maternal" without appearing "hysterical," to be affectionate but not invasive. We can attest to the pressure of stereotypes and the absence of female role models to help with personal development in the workplace. However, new styles are emerging: women who are intelligent and elegant, persistent, better listeners. Like Seneca said, these are favorable winds for those who know where they are going. They are moving from "reactive" to "proactive" attitudes. They do not act on impulse, but through reflection and strategic planning.

When to be merciless or exercise authority.   In comments about their management style, some women said they were "worse than a man," reflecting an awareness that there are still many matters pending resolution in upper management. These comments can prove paralyzing for people who receive them. There is a great difference between exercising authority and being authoritarian. Whoever is authoritarian, whether man or woman, and goes around shouting at others, immediately loses his/her authority. Managing things peacefully grants one credibility. There is a certain fear of exercising one's power, as if at a subconscious level she needed to ask for permission.

Women outside work

In broad terms women have fewer social spaces. Soccer matches, a drink with friends at a bar – these are all spaces where men consolidate networks and close deals. Women do not yet have similar spaces. We don't see the habit of professionally recommending a female colleague. There are few spaces for the creation of networks, recommendations and such, and when it does happen, it is strongly criticized by men.

Meetings between women are necessary as a way to exchange emotional issues. Personal life has a stronger influence on them than men, and they need to talk about what is happening to them. The develop-

ment of professional networks is not an imperative yet, and there is resistance to creating spaces for women's professional advancement.

Women also cannot get themselves admitted into male networks (soccer, drinks, golf...) They feel like outsiders when they try to, although there are a few cases.

The partner: support or burden

The concepts of "bachelor" and "old maid" are gone and replaced with "singles." But there is still an important need to share one's life and affections, to create bonds in order to better deal with a society that is increasingly demanding of individuals. A partner can help a woman take off (in a minority of cases) although he can also be a burden because of the demands he places on her. These are completely new situations, examples of which are found in our study. Among the younger women with a partner and small children, there is a negotiation over who will act as provider depending on the demands and possibilities of the labor market. The change of roles is disconcerting. Older married women sometimes have partners of a retirement age and, depending on their personal hobbies, these men can turn into a burden. At this point in their lives, men must deconstruct their own socialization.

Living with guilt or overcoming it

There is still the pending matter of women feeling guilty for not living up to all the expectations. They feel pulled in several directions. If they had children, and if the children are all grown up, they are still asked for constant availability. Now comes the time to care for their elderly parents. Social demands regarding women's commitment to caregiving are much higher than for men. How this matter is resolved depends a great deal on social context. In some cases it is frowned upon not to care for the elderly oneself, while in other cases it's the other way around, with society or nursing homes taking over this job. Only if women stop thinking about others and acknowledge their right to enjoy life will they stop feeling guilty.

The male perspective

Since men have been socialized with a focus on their role as providers, sometimes they do not perceive the benefits of change, just

their "loss of place," which is to say a loss of centrality. They experience women's advancement as a threat. And since what is at stake is power, these benefits are much harder to share. This is no longer about sharing laundry duties but about sharing real power, and this power is located in economic circles, where the presence of women is still scarce. Men, on the other hand, are ill-prepared for emotional behavior, which makes it difficult for them to understand what is happening to them internally. They have a lot more trouble accepting change. Now it is men's turn to break with the past, because the rules of the game have changed.

At the biological and emotional levels, there is a wall of silence around male menopause. It is something to be feared, but not talked about. The fact of not procreating makes it harder for them to understand the realities of life, and this makes them feel an irrational fear of aging, death and other types of loss. For women, the crisis point in their life cycle begins when their commitment needs to be at a maximum, and they are faced with a choice. Men, on the contrary, can enjoy a linear development. Men's crisis coincides with the midlife crisis resulting from biological changes and, for executives, the fact of not having developed other interests. Men can also choose to change their priorities.

Our study detected two types of men. The egalitarians wish to share with women the pleasures of rearing children or cooking food, even the less pleasurable household chores. They see women as people with equal rights and obligations. The traditionalists do not tolerate women going from "admirers" to "competitors." When this happens, they sometimes switch to a younger woman. It does not cross their minds to take on tasks generally considered to be feminine, nor to act as real partners, as that would raise questions about their masculinity.

By not being in touch with their own feelings, it is difficult for them to display them, to accept the passage of time or to exteriorize their feelings. This creates negatives health effects on themselves and on the other members of the family, especially the sons, who notice these shortcomings and the lack of a male role model.

Many men are still trapped in the role of the material provider, not the provider of affection. They hold on to the expectations generated by the myth of masculinity, and give themselves little leeway

to develop and to show their emotional side, putting work concerns ahead of family concerns. In other words, they prioritize their schedules, but they do not schedule their priorities.

For men, family time is more limited. Their minds did not create spaces for relaxation. They are to a great extent the product of socialization.

The time they do find to develop other interests is almost always linked to the creation of networks. This shortage of hobbies negatively conditions the period of retirement. Women, on the contrary, take courses that lead to personal development.

Men are more familiar with power. They tend to perform few tasks that are not profitable in economic terms. They prioritize economic security over emotional security. While women underestimate their own power, men overestimate theirs.

Men do not generally have a mental picture of the female manager. They associate women with the roles of mother and wife. They are attracted by the qualities of a "dependent little girl." When a woman is assertive and independent, she is said to be "unfeminine." Intellectual capacity is considered a male territory and is devaluated and ridiculed when it appears in women.

Fathers: what models to propose

As fathers, men can compensate for their loss of leadership at work by creating new roles for themselves besides that of provider. Getting in touch with their emotional side brings experiences that enables them to evolve from being a controlling boss – a hallmark of the industrial age – to a facilitator of his colleagues' potential. New fathers are aware of the importance of their presence in building their children's social identity. Our interviewees admitted to a marked absence during the first years of their children's lives, but an important presence in later years.

The men that decide to enjoy their paternity see their children as engineers of happiness, because they help them move from a selfish outlook on life to a broader, more mature viewpoint. In short, they learn that happiness can be much greater through giving (in this case, through children) instead of receiving. Participating in child rearing is an experience that affects all sides of life, both personally and professionally. Shared maternity/paternity can influence maternal and paternal images, and make children become people who are

able to interact with others from a more open, egalitarian and respectful way.

Bosses: getting admiration vs promoting/mentoring

New leaders are replacing the "I give the orders around here" attitude and the search for admiration with a more egalitarian style of management. Insofar as bonds of confidence can be developed, executives can delegate and enjoy other sides of life. Mentors display a benevolent differentiation by virtue of which men act in a protective, paternalist way to "protect and care for women." The more advanced ones manage to help their colleagues find their own voice.

Equals: overcoming mistrust and stereotypes

If men can overcome their distrust of women, they will stop viewing their success as an indication that they are not men enough to take care of their families, and instead revise their distribution of time and roles. Men tend to hold the belief that women attach too much importance to emotional bonds, and don't consider the company "a great game," instead of perceiving this emotional intelligence as a growing value in today's organization.

Equal or better

A few interviewees had positive opinions on women's working capacity. They valued having them as colleagues, but noticed a transformation when women took on power roles, which sometimes led to emotional attacks and resulted in their being branded as "hysterical." These men strongly criticized women when they felt the latter were trying to imitate men.

Conversely, they observed a complementary gender differentiation according to which women are in possession of positive traits that complement male traits. This admission is linked to the need for women to care for their children.

Motherhood is just a phase

Being a mother is no longer the main goal of a woman's life. But it seems that men are not yet aware of the new place occupied by motherhood. Women have limited their own functions and men are not ready to take over. We observed a constant belief among male managers that motherhood is a lifelong endeavor. If women

give up their careers, they will be excluded for years from any chance of progress.

The company has to contribute something

The company or the business owner see motherhood as purely a female concern, without any need for the company to assist her in any way. This makes companies lose valuable assets at a time when there is a shortage of talent. Nowhere do we see a social responsibility on the part of the company on this point. Changing paradigms and negotiating maternity leave would be more profitable in economic terms for the firm. The fear of not being hired on the candidate's part and the lack of flexibility on the firm's part create negative results for both parties.

Subordinates.   From their roles as subordinates we built a list of men's attitudes towards female managers ranging from:

a) hostile behavior towards female bosses, symbolized by a paternal attitude that considers women inferior, thus justifying their domination,
b) competitive differentiation according to which women do not have the necessary skills to work in the business world and should thus remain in the private sphere,
c) differentiation based on the danger posed by women who are "manipulative and dangerous," intrusive when they step over bounds and wish to take control over men's tasks.

In short, some men display all their aggressiveness before a potential "loss of centrality;" they get on the defensive and view women's new position as a threat. Devaluation is a constant theme.

We observed that many male executives are uncomfortable when a female colleague is in charge. However, they respect older women more as professionals. Beauty becomes secondary and these women are respected for their skills.

But younger men say that women bosses are better, because they do not need to be permanently asserting their authority and do not mince their words when they are praising a job well done. A good working atmosphere means less job rotation and emotional and material benefits.

The persistence of certain gender stereotypes creates enormous pressure for men and women. The man can feel trapped in his role as provider, while the woman is caught in the confusion between social expectations and personal desires. There is a lot of self-applied pressure and a lot of outside pressure to live up to the prevailing ideals of beauty. There is little discrimination between the different stages of the life cycle, especially the motherhood stage. Women struggle in a sea of fear, guilt and low self-esteem, which hinders the creation of bonds and networks built on solidarity. Sometimes, women are their own worst enemies. Besides real advances in the workplace, access to upper management requires greater thought on external limitations, but especially on internal limitations that we tried to deconstruct in this study. It would be highly relevant to contrast our insights with an empirical, quantitative study.

Appendix

Outline for group discussions

1. How do you feel at this stage in your life?
   Explore levels
   - Emotional
   - Professional, etc.
2. What do you consider the factors behind your professional success?
3. What obstacles did you find at the workplace on your way to the top?
   Explore
   - Mentors/networks
   - Motherhood
   - Couple (in connection with professional growth – cooperation or competition)
   - Emotions
   - Reconciling work and family
4. Although there are fewer external obstacles these days, the percentage of women in upper management is still low. Why do you think that is? Could there be internal obstacles in their path?
   - Low self-esteem
   - Too much flexibility
   - Spoken and body language
   - Less ambitious
   - Not asking anything for themselves
   - Less time, etc.
5. What messages do you remember as having the greatest impact on you?
   - Work
   - Family
   - Father/mother
   - Books
   - Socialization

Outline for in-depth interviews

The interview moves from the present to the past, from "now" to "then."

1. Working life

In order to provide some context, how long have you been (name person's position)? I would like you to tell me about your career development, about how you got here. Tell me about the most important and decisive moments, how events in your personal life influenced your career...Start wherever you like, and we can go into greater detail later.

2. Representation of working life

Was this road or process more or less a conscious one for you? In other words, was it the result of calculated decisions, of taking opportunities, of luck...?
Were you clear about what you wanted when you started out?
Did you have to make major decisions? I don't mean decisions about specific aspects of your job, but decisions that affected your personal and professional lives. (If one is mentioned) Why was it important?
Did you have examples to follow, guides, role models, figures to inspire you?
Did you have a clear goal? Do you now?
During your college and graduate school years, what were the expectations of the other students of your generation? What were the ideals for male and for female students?
What messages did you receive back then that had a deep influence on you and which do you still remember? (introduce more specific questions if nothing has emerged yet)
What were the determining factors for your professional success?
What were the roles played by precollege education and college education?
Did you pursue a master's degree? In Spain or abroad? How important was it?
Was there any one person who had a special influence over your career?
What are your strong points as a manager? Your weak points?

What do you like about being a male/female manager? What don't you like?

3. The female manager/the male manager

Based on your experience and what you know about other colleagues, do you think there are differences between a man and a woman's career as an executive? What are they? How do you think men experience these differences as opposed to women? (if women do not respond, make suggestions) What differences do you see along the road traveled by men and women managers?

- In the family
- In education (school, college, graduate school...)
- At work

What are a man's advantages? What are a woman's advantages?
What obstacles does a man face? And a woman?
What does a woman bring to a organization's structure?
What is the influence of new interest groups (clients, shareholders, employees, etc.) on the promotion of women in the workplace?
In your own case, how do your male colleagues see you? What about women: are you a role model or a rival?
Is the role of women at the workplace changing?
Do you think that men and women have different managing styles?
(IF SHE DOES NOT OWN HER OWN COMPANY) Did you ever consider creating your own business? Why not?
(IF SHE OWNS HER OWN COMPANY) What prompted you to create your own business?

4. The female manager: relationships and emotions

Going back to a more personal level...Do you feel that you left something behind on your road to the top? What? (Let her talk at length)
If you could start all over would you change anything?
How is your personal life compared with your work life? Explore all levels:

- Couple
- Children
- Group of friends
- Work colleagues

Insist on:

Couple: the role of wife/partner/role distribution

- Assessment
- Evolution throughout the years (herself alone and with her partner)
- Problems/satisfaction
- Competitiveness/understanding/cooperation

What do you ask of your partner?

- Family life: the role of mother/caregiver
- Children: what they bring, what they demand, etc.
- Care, dedication, demands, listening, etc.
- Time spent out of the house
- Guilt, rewards, etc.
- Other relatives: parents, in-laws, etc.

5. Female manager: messages from childhood and adolescence

Let us go back to your childhood and move forward from there.
Find out specific details about:
Do you have any brothers?
What do your parents do?
How influential were your father/mother/siblings on your career choice?
What messages do you remember from your childhood and teenage years? What was expected of you? Are these messages different from those received by your brothers?
Specific messages related to money. Learning to save and manage money, but not to be providers, attitude towards risk.

Figure A.1   **Theories about Women in Management**

TOKEN THEORY	QUEEN BEE SYNDROME	SHOWCASE WOMAN	THEORIES OF DIVERSITY
ROSABETH MOSS KANTER	SARRIÓ / BURIN	NAOMI WOLF / G. FERRANDO	SIMMEL/ DURKHEIM
Supress differences	• Lack of gender awareness	• Adding modern touch to the profession or job	HOFFSTEDE. Mental software
↓	• Avoiding talking in favour of somebody	• "Beauty myth"	GILLIGAN/ CORIA/TOBIO
• Minority group	• They prefer to be the only ones	• Sexuality in organizations	DE ANCA/ VAZQUEZ VEGA
• Fear of failure			Promote differences = creativity and talent

Source: Produced by author

Figure A.2   **Gender Identity Differences**

	MEN	WOMEN
FEAR	Of failing	Of rejection
NEED FOR	Separation	Connection
ORIENTATION	Towards oneself Selfishness	Others Altruism
FAMILY SOCIALIZATION	Working role	Diversity of roles
WORK EVOLUTION	Continuity	Discontinuity
ORGANIZATIONAL BEHAVIOR	More action, decision	More emotion, environment
WORK PRIORITIES	Money, competition, getting to the top	Amusement, integration, agreeable work environment

Source: Produced by author

Figure A.3 **Analysis Results Chart – Arguments of Women Managers and Life Cycle I**

LEVEL	30–45 YEARS OLD	46–60 YEARS OLD
SOCIAL	• Pressure from environment • Sexuality comes first • Beauty is highly valued	• Less pressure from environment • Sexuality is not a priority • Abilities are valued. Invisible
FAMILY	• Working mothers • Rivalry with brothers • Absent fathers • Indifference • Little financial socialization	• Work is not encouraged • Brothers are more highly valued • Late paternal encouragement • Devaluation • No financial socialization
COUPLE	• No couple • Delay in maternity • No maternity	• Rivalry with couple • Divorces • Conflicts

Source: Produced by author

Figure A.4 **Analysis Results Chart – Arguments of Women Managers and Life Cycle II**

LEVEL	30–45 YEARS OLD	46–60 YEARS OLD
ACCESS TO LABOR MARKET	• Women are confused • Hard to resolve	• Easy to access the workplace • Difficult to get to the top
ORGANIZA-TION	• Competitive • MBA and networks • Fear of using power	• Cooperative • In the middle, not the top • Fear of being rejected
WORK PLACE IDENTITY	• Demands a lot of herself • Selfish • Motherhood no longer a priority • Need for a new identity. Anxiety	• Demands a lot of herself • Always giving others • Post – maternity : new opportunity • Basics of identity : ease

Source: Produced by author

Figure A.5 **Analysis Results Chart – Arguments of Women Managers and Life Cycle III**

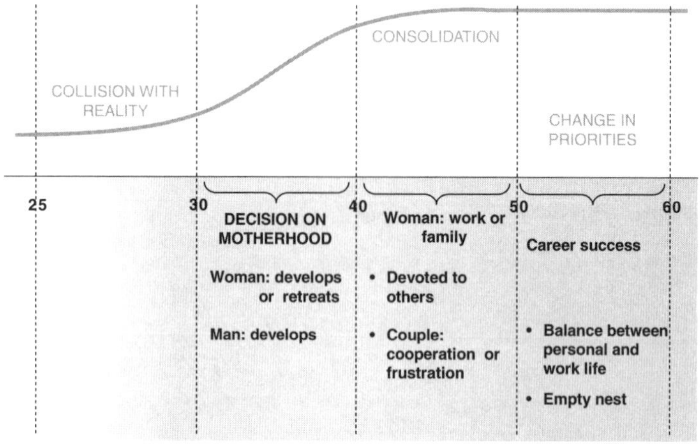

CONSOLIDATION

COLLISION WITH
REALITY

CHANGE IN
PRIORITIES

25   30   40   50   60

**DECISION ON
MOTHERHOOD**

Woman: work or
family

Career success

**Woman: develops
or retreats**

• **Devoted to
others**

Man: develops

• **Couple:
cooperation or
frustration**

• **Balance between
personal and
work life**

• **Empty nest**

Source: Produced by author

Figure A.6 **Content Analysis of Discourses. Conflict Between Altruism and Selfishness**

• The more maternal you are, the
more feminine

• Motherhood: unconditional love,
generosity without personal
interests

• Conflicts when own interests
are prioritized, or when you ask
for a higher salary

Source: Produced by author

Figure A.7 **Analysis Results – Female Managers and Money**

Source: Produced by author

Figure A.8 **Analysis Results – Female Managers and Motherhood**

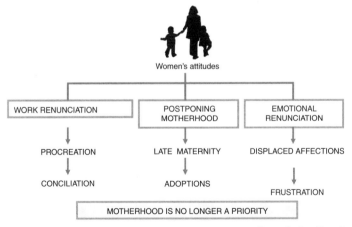

Source: Produced by author

Figure A.9 **Types of Male Arguments**

EGALITARIANS	TRADITIONALISTS
1. They want to share spaces instead of competing. Role diversity.	1. Fear of feminine competition. Fear of losing centrality. Unique role of breadwinner.
2. Experience of fatherhood from the beginning. Changing roles.	2. Exercise of fatherhood in post-adolescence.
3. Socialization as material and affection provider. Liberated.	3. Socialization as the breadwinner. Trapped.

Source: Produced by author

Figure A.10 **Male Arguments and Attitudes Towards Women's Development**

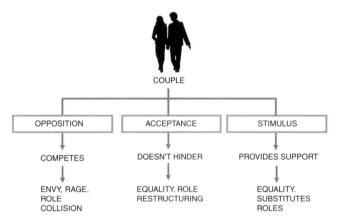

Source: Produced by author

Figure A.11 **Male Arguments and Attitudes Towards Women Managers**

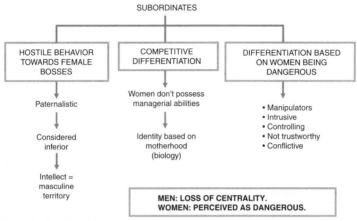

Source: Produced by author

Notes

1   Kets de Vries, M. *La organización neurótica* (The Neurotic Organisation), Barcelona, Editorial Apóstrofe, 1993.
2   Moss Kanter, R. *Men and Women of the Corporation*. New York, Basic Books, 1977.
3   Sarrió, M. *Barreras y condicionantes en la igualdad de las organizaciones*. Unpublished paper.
4   Bingham, M. and Stryker, S. *Things will be different for my daughter*. Middlesex, Penguin Books, 1995.
5   Sánchez Appelániz, M. *Mujeres, dirección y cultura organizacional*. Madrid, CIS/FEDEPE, 1997.
6   Infoempleo. *Mujer y empleo: opciones y decisiones*, 2006.
7   Hymowitz, C. "The glass wall," women are succeeding in executive ranks but mostly in selected industries. *The Wall Street Journal*, 6 February 2006.
8   "The importance of sex." Forget China, India and the Internet: economic growth is driven by women. *The Economist*, April 2006.
9   Lyness, K. and Thompson, D. "Climbing the corporate ladder: Do female and male executives follow the same route?," in American Psychological Association, Vol. 85, 2000, *Journal of Applied Psychology*.
10   Fischlmayr, Iris C. "Female self-perception as a barrier to an international career," in *International Journal of Human Resource Management*, Vol. 13, No. 5, August 2002, pp. 773–783.
11   Pérez Adán, José et al. *Cine y sociedad. Prácticas de las Ciencias Sociales*. Madrid, Ediciones Universitarias Internacionales.
12   Rifkin, J. *La era del acceso* (The Age of Access). Barcelona, Paidós, 2000.
13   Miller. "La organización saludable," in *Estudios de Administración*, Vol. 5, No. 2, 1998.
14   Covey, S. *El octavo hábito*. Barcelona, Paidós, 2005.
15   Zygmunt Bauman. *Identidad*. Madrid, Editorial Losada, 2005.
16   Sennett, R. *La corrosión del carácter*. Madrid, Anagrama, 2004.
17   Piñuel, I. *Mobbing, cómo sobrevivir al acoso psicológico en el trabajo*. Santander, Editorial Sal Terrae, 2001.
18   Piñuel, I. *Neomanagement. Jefes tóxicos y sus víctimas*. Madrid, Aguilar, 2004.
19   Rifkin, J. *La era del acceso*. Barcelona, Paidós, 2004.
20   Dupuy, F. *La fatiga de las élites. El capitalismo y sus ejecutivos*. Buenos Aires, Ediciones Manantial, 2005.
21   Gilligan, C. *In a Different Voice*. Cambridge, Harvard University Press, 1993.
22   Wolf, N. *Misconceptions*. London, Vintage, Random House, 1994.

23 Total event in the sense provided by L. Strauss. An event that affects all aspects of society, in this case of a woman. Once a woman has had a child no aspect of her personality can be understood completely without taking this into account.

24 Durán, María Ángeles (ed.) *Mujeres y hombres en la formación de la teoría sociológica.* Madrid, CIS, Colección Academia, 1996.

25 Kets de Vries, M. *La conducta del directivo.* Bilbao, Deusto, 1996.

26 Alderfer, C.P. "An intergroup perspective in group dynamics," in J. Lorsch (ed.) *Handbook of organizational behaviour.* Englewood Cliffs, N.J., Prentice Hall, 1986.

27 Requena Santos. *Redes sociales y mercado de trabajo.* Madrid, Monografías CIS, 1991.

28 Lope, A., Lozares, C. and Miguélez, F. "Perspectivas de análisis y primeros resultados de una investigación entre formación y empleo". REIS, 1997, 77–78.

29 Perrow, C. "Small firm networks". Unpublished paper.

30 Coria, C. et al. *Los cambios en la vida de las mujeres: Temores, mitos y estrategias.* Buenos Aires, Paidós, 2005.

31 Ferrando, G. *Postmodernidad y deporte: Entre la individualidad y la masificación.* Madrid. Consejo Superior de Deportes y Centro de Investigaciones Sociológicas, 2006.

32 Wolf, N. *The beauty myth.* London, Random House, 1994.

33 Levinson, D. *The seasons of a man's life.* New York, Ballantine Books, 1978.

34 Sheehy, G. *Transiciones.* Barcelona, Urano, 1999.

35 Wolf, N. *Misconceptions.* London, Random House, 1994.

36 Touraine, A. *Un nuevo paradigma para comprender el mundo de hoy.* Buenos Aires, Paidós, 2006.

37 Giddens, A. *La identidad en el mundo contemporáneo.* Barcelona, Península, 1995.

38 Covey, S. *Los siete hábitos de la gente altamente efectiva.* Barcelona, Paidós, 2004.

39 Senett, R. *El respeto: sobre la dignidad del hombre en un mundo de desigualdad.* Madrid, Anagrama, 2003.

40 CIS data. Study no. 2126.

41 García Ferrando, M. *Posmodernidad y deporte: Entre la individuación y la masificación.* Madrid, Consejo Superior de Deportes y Centro de Investigaciones Sociológicas, 2006.

42 Bañuelos, C. "Los patrones estéticos en los albores del siglo XXI. Hacia una revisión en los estudios en torno a este tema". Madrid CIS, REIS no. 68.

43 Grinberg. *Culpa y depresión.* Barcelona, Paidós, 2002.

44 Coria, C. op. cit.

45 Covey, S. *Lo primero es lo primero.* Buenos Aires, Paidós, 1995.

46 Tobio, C. "Dilemas y estrategias de las madres que trabajan," in Casado Aparicio, E. and Gómez Esteban, C. *Los desafíos de la conciliación de la vida familiar y profesional en el siglo XXI.* Madrid, Fundación Ortega y Gassett, Editorial Biblioteca Nueva, 2006.

47   Dolto, F. *La dificultad de vivir*. Buenos Aires, Gedisa, 1981.
48   Neugarten, D. *Sexuality in organisations: romantic and coercive behaviours*. Illinois, More Publishing Co., 1990.
49   Sarrió, M. *La psicología del género a través del techo de cristal*. Valencia, Bancaixa, 2004.
50   Freud, S. *Malestar en la cultura*. Buenos Aires, Amorrortu, 1990.
51   Op. cit.
52   Covey, S. *Los siete hábitos de la gente altamente efectiva*. Barcelona, Paidós, 2004.
53   Tobio, C. op. cit.
54   Coria, C. et al. op. cit. "Los cambios en la vida de las mujeres..." pp. 31–32.
55   Babcock, L. and Laschever, S. *Las mujeres no se atreven a pedir: saber negociar es cosa de hombres*. Barcelona, Amat Editorial, 2005.
56   Fischlmayr, Iris C. "Female self-perception as a barrier to an international career," in *International Journal of Human Resource Management*. August 2002, pp. 773–783.
57   Covey, S. *Los siete hábitos de la gente...* op. cit.
58   Bion, W. *Experiencias en grupos*. Buenos Aires, Paidós, 1995. Working group refers to the ability to communicate, to cooperate, to not feel emotionally overwhelmed, to know one's own possibilities and limitations, all of which comes up time and again when talking about the time variable.
59   Bion, W. op. cit. Basic assumption group makes reference to the most primary of emotions that invade a person, making him or her incapable of thinking or cooperating. Behavior turns to fight or flight mode. These are gut behaviors.
60   Burin, M. and Meler, I. *Varones: género y subjetividad masculina*. Barcelona, Paidós, 2000.
61   Burin and Meler op. cit.
62   Sennett, R. *El respeto: sobre la dignidad del hombre en un mundo de desigualdad*. Madrid, Anagrama, 2003.
63   Zygmunt Bauman, *Identidad*. Madrid, Losada, 2005.
64   Sheehy, G. *Transiciones: comprender las fases de la madurez en la vida de los hombres*. Barcelona, Urano 1999.
65   Ibarra, H. "Differences in men and women's access to informal networks at work: An intergroup perspective". Paper presented at Academy of Management. San Francisco, 2000.
66   Idem. Earlier op. cit.
67   Piñuel, I. Neomanagement. *Jefes tóxicos y sus víctimas*. Madrid, Aguilar, 2004.
68   Touraine, A. *Los nuevos paradigmas sociales*, op. cit.
69   Sheehy, G. *Transiciones*. op. cit.
70   Sheehy, G. *Transiciones*. op. cit.
71   Shefrin, H. *Más allá del miedo y la codicia*. México, Oxford University Press, 2000.
72   Dowling, C. *El complejo de cenicienta*. Buenos Aires, Grijalbo, 1982.

73 Sheehy, G. *Transiciones.* op. cit.
74 Coria, C. *Las negociaciones nuestras de cada día.* Buenos Aires, Paidós, 2003.
75 Babcock, L. and Laschever, S. *Las mujeres no se atreven a pedir.* Barcelona, Amat, 2005.
76 Kiyosaki et al. *Padre rico, padre pobre.* Buenos Aires, Time and Money Publications, 2001.
77 Ibarra, H. "Differences in men's and women's access to informal networks at work: An intergroup perspective". Paper presented at the Academy of Management, San Francisco, 2000.
78 Requena Santos. *Redes sociales y mercado de trabajo.* Madrid, CIS, Monography No. 119, 1991.
79 Coria, C. *El dinero en la pareja: algunas desnudeces sobre el poder.* Buenos Aires, Paidós, 1998.
80 Forward, S. *Chantaje emocional.* Barcelona, Martínez Roca, 1999.
81 Hegelsen, S. *The female advantage.* New York, Doubleday, 1995.
82 Lope, A., Lozares, C. and Miguélez, F. "Perspectivas de análisis y primeros resultados de una investigación sobre la relación entre formación y empleo". REIS, 77–78, 1997, pp. 283–305.
83 Barbera, E. *Género y diversidad en un entorno de cambio.* Valencia, Universidad Politécnica, 2005.
84 Mintzberg, H. *Directivos, no MBAs, una visión crítica de la dirección de empresas y formación empresarial.* Bilbao, Deusto, 2005.
85 Sennett, R. *The corrosion of character: The consequences of work in the new capitalism.* London, Norton, 1999.
86 Almagro, J.J. *Jefes, jefecillos y jefazos.* Madrid, Pearson Educación, 2005.
87 Sennett, R. *The corrosion of character.* op. cit.
88 Useem, M. *The Inner Circle.* New York, Oxford University Press, 1984.
89 Rifkin, J. *La era del acceso.* Barcelona, Paidós, 2000.
90 Kaufmann, A. et al. "El coste psicológico de las fusiones y absorciones," in *Construir equipos de trabajo en la era de la conexión.* Obra Social Caja Madrid, Alcalá, 2003.
91 Kaufmann, A. "Analfabetismo o inteligencia emocional en la empresa española," in *Construir equipos ...* op. cit.
92 Sennett, R. *The corrosion of character.* London, Norton, 1998.
93 Bauman, Z. *Identidad.* Barcelona, Losada, 2005.
94 Daniel, C. "Posibilidades y limitaciones de los equipos virtuales," in *Construir equipos de trabajo en la era de la conexión,* op. cit.
95 Levinson, D. *The seasons of a man's life.* Ballantine Books, New York, 1978.
96 Sheehy, G. op. cit.
97 Kets de Vries, M. *La organización neurótica.* Barcelona, Editorial Apóstrofe, 1993.
98 Durán, M.A. (ed.) *Mujeres y hombres en la formación de la teoría sociológica.* Madrid, CIS, Colección Academia, 1997.

 99 Alberdi, I. "Parsons: el funcionalismo y la idealización de la división sexual del trabajo," in *Mujeres y hombres en la teoría...* op. cit.
100 Mintzberg, H. *Directivos, no MBAs*. Bilbao, Deusto, 2005.
101 Catherine Valabregue et al. *Ces maternités que l'on dit tardives*. Paris, Laffont, 1990.

Bibliography

Alberdi, I. "Parsons: el funcionalismo y la idealización de la división sexual del trabajo," in *Mujeres y hombres en la teoría sociológica*. Madrid, CIS, Colección Academia, 1997.

Alberoni, E. *Los envidiosos*. Barcelona, Gedisa, 1991.

Alderfer, C.P. "An intergroup perspective in group dynamics," in J. Lorsch (ed.) *Handbook of organizational behaviour*. Englewood Cliffs, N.J., Prentice Hall, 1986.

Almagro, J.J. *Jefes, jefecillos y jefazos*. Madrid, Pearson Educación, 2005.

Babcock, L. and Laschever, S. *Las mujeres no se atreven a pedir: saber negociar es cosa de hombres*. Barcelona, Amat Editorial, 2005.

Bañuelos, C. "Los patrones estéticos en los albores del siglo XXI. Hacia una revisión en los estudios en torno a este tema". Madrid CIS, REIS no. 68.

Barbera, E. *Género y diversidad en un entorno de cambio*. Valencia, Universidad Politécnica, 2005.

Bauman, Z. *Identidad*. Barcelona, Losada, 2005.

Berg, D. et al. *The self in social inquiry: research methods*. London, Sage, 1988.

Bingham, M. and Stryker, S. *Things will be different for my daughter*. Middlesex, Penguin Books, 1995.

Bion, W. *Experiencias en grupos*. Buenos Aires, Paidós, 1995.

Burín, M. *Estudios sobre la subjetividad femenina*. Grupo Editor Latinoamericano, Buenos Aires, 1987.

Burin, M. and Meler, I. *Varones: género y subjetividad masculina*. Barcelona, Paidós, 2000.

Catherine Valabregue et al. *Ces maternités que l'on dit tardives*. Paris, Laffont, 1990.

CIS data. Study no. 2126.

Coria, C. et al. *Los cambios en la vida de las mujeres: Temores, mitos y estrategias*. Buenos Aires, Paidós, 2005.

Coria, C. *El dinero en la pareja: algunas desnudeces sobre el poder*. Buenos Aires, Paidós, 1998.

Coria, C. *El sexo oculto del dinero*. Formas de la dependencia femenina. Barcelona, Paidós, 1997.

Coria, C. *Las negociaciones nuestras de cada día*. Buenos Aires, Paidós, 2003.

Covey, S. *Lo primero es lo primero*. Buenos Aires, Paidós, 1995.

Covey, S. *Los siete hábitos de la gente altamente efectiva*. Barcelona, Paidós, 2004.

Covey, S. *Los 7 hábitos de la gente altamente efectiva*. Buenos Aires, Paidós, 2005.

Covey, S. *El octavo hábito*. Barcelona, Paidós, 2005.

Daniel, C. "Posibilidades y limitaciones de los equipos virtuales," in *Construir equipos de trabajo en la era de la conexión* by A. Kaufmann et al.

De Anca, C. and Vazquez Vega, A. *La gestión de la diversidad en la organización*. Madrid, Prentice, May, 2005. (Available in English).

Díaz Martínez, Capitolina et al. *Dinero, amor e individualización. Las relaciones económicas en las parejas/familias contemporáneas*. Oviedo, Instituto Asturiano de la mujer, 2005.

Dolto, F. *La dificultad de vivir*. Buenos Aires, Gedisa, 1981.

Domínguez, J. and Robin, V. *La bolsa o la vida*. Barcelona, Planeta, 1997.

Dowling, C. *El complejo de cenicienta*. Buenos Aires, Grijalbo, 1982.

Dupuy, F. *La fatiga de las élites. El capitalismo y sus ejecutivos*. Buenos Aires, Ediciones Manantial, 2005.

Duran, María Ángeles (ed.). *Mujeres y hombres en la formación de la teoría sociológica*. Madrid, CIS, Colección Academia, 1996.

Fisher, Marc. *El regalo del millonario*. Barcelona, Nuevos emprendedores, 2002.

Fischlmayr, Iris C. "Female self-perception as a barrier to an international career," in *International Journal of Human Resource Management*. August 2002, pp. 773–783.

Forward, S. *Chantaje emocional*. Barcelona, Martínez Roca, 1999.

Freud, Sigmund. *Malestar en la cultura*. Buenos Aires, Amorrortu, 1992.

García Ferrando, M. *Posmodernidad y deporte: Entre la individuación y la masificación*. Madrid, Consejo Superior de Deportes y Centro de Investigaciones Sociológicas, 2006.

Garmendia, J.A. *Tres culturas: organización y RRHH*. Madrid, Esic, 1994.

Gawain, S. *Descubra la verdadera prosperidad*. Barcelona, Plaza & Janés, 1997.

Giddens, A. *La identidad en el mundo contemporáneo*. Barcelona, Península, 1995.

Gilligan, C. *In a Different Voice*. Cambridge, Harvard University Press, 1995.

Grinberg, L. *Culpa y depresión*. Barcelona, Paidos, 2002.

Hegelsen, S. *The female advantage*. New York, Doubleday, 1995.

Hymowitz, C. "The glass wall," women are succeeding in executive ranks but mostly in selected industries. *The Wall Street Journal*. 6 February 2006.

Ibarra, H. "Differences in men's and woman's access to informal networks at work: An intergroup perspective". Paper presented at Academy of Management. San Francisco, 2000.

Infoempleo. *Mujer y empleo: opciones y decisiones*, 2006.

Kaufmann, A. *Líder global, en la vida y en la empresa*. Madrid, Ediciones Universidad de Alcalá, 1999.

Kaufmann, A. and De Prado, M. *Construir equipos en la era de la conexión*. Madrid, Universidad de Alcalá y Caja Madrid, 2003.

Kaufmann, A. et al. "El coste psicológico de las fusiones y absorciones," in *Construir equipos de trabajo en la era de la conexión*. Obra Social Caja Madrid, Alcalá, 2003.

Kets de Vries, M. *La conducta del directivo*. Bilbao, Deusto, 1996.

Kets de Vries, M. *La organización neurótica*. Barcelona, Editorial Apóstrofe, 1993.

Kiyosaki, et al. *Padre rico, padre pobre*. Buenos Aires, Time and Money Publications, 2001.

Levinson, D. *The seasons of a man's life*. New York, Ballantine Books, 1978.

Lope, A., Lozares, C. and Mígueles, F. "Perspectivas de análisis y primeros resultados de una investigación entre formación y empleo". REIS, 1997, 77–78.

Lyness, K. and Thompson, D. "Climbing the corporate ladder: Do female and male executives follow the same route?," in American Psychological Association, Vol. 85, 2000, *Journal of Applied Psychology*.

Miller. "La organización saludable," in *Estudios de Administración*, Vol. 5, No. 2, 1998.

Mintzberg, H. *Directivos, no MBAs, una visión crítica de la dirección de empresas y formación empresarial*. Bilbao, Deusto, 2005.

Moss Kanter, R. *Men and Woman of the Corporation*. New York, Basic Books, 1977.

Moss Kanter, R. *Las nuevas fronteras del management*. Barcelona, Piados, 1997.

Needleman, *El dinero y el sentido de la vida*. Madrid, Temas de Hoy, 1991.

Neugarten, D. *Sexuality in organisations: romantic and coercive behaviours*. Illinois, More Publishing Co., 1990.

Pérez Adán, José et al. *Cine y sociedad. Prácticas de las Ciencias Sociales*. Madrid, Ediciones Universitarias Internacionales.

Perrow, C. *Small firm networks*. Unpublished paper.

Piñuel, I. *Mobbing, cómo sobrevivir al acoso psicológico en el trabajo*. Santander, Editorial Sal Terrae, 2001.

Piñuel, I. *Neomanagement: Jefes Tóxicos y sus víctimas*. Madrid, Aguilar, 2004.

Requena Santos. *Redes sociales y mercado de trabajo*. Madrid, CIS, Monography No. 119, 1991.

Ritzer. *La Mc Donalización de la sociedad*. Barcelona, Ariel, 1996.

Rifkin, J. *La era del acceso* (The Age of Access). Barcelona, Paidós, 2000.

Sánchez Apellániz, Mercedes. *Mujeres, dirección y cultura organizacional*. Madrid, CIS /FEDEPE, 1997.

Sarrió, et al. "Mujeres directivas, espacio de poder y relaciones de género," in *Anuario de Psicología*, Vol. 34, No. 2, 2003.

Sarrió, M. *Barreras y condicionantes en la igualdad de las organizaciones*. Unpublished paper.

Sarrió, M. *La psicología del género a través del techo de cristal*. Valencia, Bancaixa, 2004.

Sennett, R. *The corrosion of character: The consequences of work in the new capitalism*. London, Norton, 1998.

Sennett, R. *El respeto: sobre la dignidad del hombre en un mundo de desigualdad*. Madrid, Anagrama, 2003.

Sheehy, G. *Transiciones: comprender las fases de la madurez en la vida de los hombres*. Barcelona, Urano, 1999.

Shefrin, Hersch. *Más allá del miedo y la codicia*. México, Oxford University Press, 2000.

Sinay, Sergio. *Ser padre es cosa de hombres*. Buenos Aires, Edición del Nuevo Extremo, 2004.

The Economist. April, 2006.

Tobio, C. "Dilemas y estrategias de las madres que trabajan," in Casado Aparicio, E. and Gómez Esteban, C. *Los desafíos de la conciliación de la vida*

familiar y profesional en el siglo XXI. Madrid, Fundación Ortega y Gasset, Editorial Biblioteca Nueva, 2006.

Touraine, A. *Un nuevo paradigma para comprender el mundo de hoy*. Buenos Aires, Paidós, 2006.

Useem, M. *The inner circle*. Oxford, University Press, 1984.

Wolf, N. *Misconceptions*. London, Random House, 1994.

Wolf, N. *The beauty myth*. London, Random House, 1994.

Wolf, N. *Fire with fire: The new female power and how to use it*. Toronto, Vintage Books, 1994.

Zelizer, V.A. *The social meaning of money*. New York, Basic Books, 1994.

Zygmunt Bauman. *Identidad*. Madrid, Editorial Losada, 2005.

Index

[Page numbers appearing in **bold** denote those containing tables]

"12 Angry Men" (film), 81
21st century organizations/modern corporations/modern companies, 17–19, 21, 23, 78, 86, 117, 130–131, 146–148
  competitiveness in, 46–47
  depersonalized relationships in, 20
  perception of motherhood of, 32–34
"24/7" dedication, 17–18, 130–131, 141

Accenture, 1
Adeslas, 13
adult life, 3, 42, 132
adults, 2, 18, 53
Aedipe (Association of Human Resources Managers), 14
affection, 71–72, 137, 141–142, 143
  and men, 127, 144–145
  women's networks of, 59, 123
Agama Consultores, 13
age groups, 14, 57, 72, 83, 132
age, xiii, 2, 14, 31, 20, 66, 73, 77, 81, 84, 113, 117, 123, 143
  of competitive workers, 46–47
  and female managers, 2, 42–45, 48–63, 78, 118–119
  hypervelocity and, 18, 141
  motherhood and, 87
aggression, 29, 52, 88, 136, 147
Alberdi, I., 135
Alderfer, C.P., 42
  intergroup dynamics, 42
Almagro, J.J., 11
altruism, xii, 76, 136 *see also* selflessness
ambiguity, 20, 90

ambition, xii, xiv, 1, 15, 58–59, 67, 85
  family influences on, 3, 106–107, 122, 133–135, 140
  of female managers, 1, 98–100, 121, 123–128, 137
  limits of, 141
  and motherhood, 137
  and promotion possibilities, 56–57, 66
  values and inhibitions in, 113–128
  and younger women, 43, 47, 138
American Association of University Women (AAUW), 8
  Shortchanging Girls, Shortchanging America (survey report findings), 8–9
anger, 11, 30
anxiety, xiv, 52, 94, 111
  21st century corporations, 1, 17–21, 49–50, 130–132
  men, 84, 88
  and women's multidimensional role, 48, 135
anxiety attacks, 38, 139
appeasement, 30, 54, 108
approval, 29, 44, 46, 51–52, 53, 55, 57, 90, 111, 132, 140
Asociación Fulbright, 13
attitudes, 1, 20, 24, 30–31, 33–34, 60, 83, 86, 107, 134, 137, 146, 147
  towards life, 62, 77
  towards money, 101–103
  proactive, 43, 54, 55, 59, 64–69, 73, 77, 140
  reactive, 64, 142
  and rejection, 89–100
  of women, 3–4, 24, 48–49, 58, 62, 71, 123

authoritarianism, 113–114, 119,
    134, 142
authority, xiv, 2, 103, 114, 120–121,
    125, 126
  women with, 45, 97, 140, 142, 147
  at workplace, 53, 91

Babcock, L., 109
Bachelet, Michelle, 45
"ball metaphor", 3, 48, 133, 137 *see
    also* other people's games
Banco Popular, 13
Banco Santander, 13
Barbera, E., 116
barriers, xiv, 101–112
Bauman, Zygmunt, 24, 131
"beauty myth", xiii, 44–45, 56, 140
behavior, 3, 11, 20, 44, 85, 88,
    91–92, 123, 130, 134, 138, 144,
    147, 161n.59
  competitiveness, 46
  dependency, 101–103, 108–113
  loneliness, 54, 94–95
  patriarchal culture, 134–135
behavioral differences, 115–116
biological identity, 27–31
Bion, W., 20, 161nn.58–59
  basic assumption groups, 20
  Tavistock model, 42
body language, 47
bonds, 27, 55, 146, 122, 130, 143,
    146
  "feminist victimism", 69–70
  mother-daughter, 53–54, 59, 61
  team works/networks, 119–120,
    123, 131–132, 148
bosses, 51, 57, 78–79, 86, 109, 120,
    123, 140, 145, 146–148
  see also female bosses
  "toxic bosses", 25
Botín, Ana Patricia, xii
Branden, Nathaniel, 75
  New Women (1993), 75
British Petroleum, 13
Burin, M., 87, 107
  "crossed identifications", 107
burnout, 20

Caja Madrid, 13
career development, 15, 33, 43, 56,
    107, 115, 133
  men's, 74–75
  women's, 3, 5, 34, 66, 76–79,
    135–140, 143
career evolution, 24, 28, 133
careers, xiv, 8–10, 34, 19, 59, 63, 74,
    107, 133, 138, 139
  and motherhood, 146–147
  and self-esteem, 7, 72
  strategy for professional
    development, 75–77
  and training in management
    skills, 136
  see also professional
    development
caregiving, xii, 3, 32, 143
change, 2, 4, 9, 23, 26–27, 36, 42,
    52, 59, 69, 86, 110, 114–115,
    123, 143, 144–145
  adaptation to, 39, 120–122
  attitudes to, 60, 137
  in corporate culture, 19–20
  globalization of society, 21,
    24–25, 48
  midlife crisis, 84
  motherhood, 29–31
  traditionalists' fears of, 88–100
childhood values, 2, 44
  influence on adult life, 42, 52–53,
    101, 132
  mental paradigms, 2, 109–113
children, xiv, 2, 28–29, 32, 49, 63,
    119, 121, 132, 134, 138–139,
    143–144, 145
  human capital, 30–31
  influences on adult life, 2, 3,
    39–40, 102, 126–127, 134
  motherhood, 37–38, 59, 63, 74,
    87–88, 135, 140
  parents' quality time with,
    35–36
  and women
    managers/entrepreneurs,
    53–58, 65, 133, 136–137,
    146

China, 21
Cinderella complex, 101–104
    ambition, 113–128
    financial socialization, 105–112
Clinton, Hillary, 45, 102
commitment, xv, 19–20, 137, 143,
    144
    of fathers, 36
    in motherhood, 32–33, 35, 47, 87,
    121
    at workplace, 27, 74, 123, 132
competitive differentiation, xiv, 147
competitive manager, 42–54
competitiveness, 29, 46, 61, 99, 107,
    134, 135–136
conditioning, 3, 63, 111, 130, 132,
    133
conduct, 4, 18, 95
conflict resolution, 3, 33, 61, 92,
    108, 143
conflicts, 42, 47, 76, 114, 118, 121,
    130, 131–132
consumer society, 2, 83, 103, 107
contacts, 1, 15, 92, 119
"containment environment", 130
Coria, C., 42, 48, 71, 103, 108, 113,
    132
    female life cycle, 42
corporate ladder, 10
couples, 4, 46, 112, 117
    divorce, 137
    motherhood, 3–4, 32–36
    unconditional support for
    partner, 99, 111
Covey, S., 44, 66
creativity, 19, 31, 56, 66–67, 76,
    101, 118–119
Crittenden, Ann, 31
    The Price of Motherhood, 31
"crossed identifications", 107, 133

Danish Embassy, 13
decision-making, xii, 123, 136,
    40
Delphi Metal, 13
dependency, 15, 19–20, 29, 47,
    62–65, 71, 126

depression, 11, 18, 30–31, 48, 52,
    53, 72, 133
Descartes, René, 17, 131
The Devil Wears Prada (film), 12
Diana, Princess, 11
differential socialization, 1, 52–53
differentiation, 24, 87, 90, 92, 135,
    147
Dircom (Association of
    Communications Managers),
    14
discrimination, xi, 32, 53, 81, 93,
    136, 140, 148
divorce/separation (marital), 15, 56,
    58, 106, 78, 113–114
Dolto, F., 51
Domínguez, J., 103
    "La bolsa o la vida" (Your purse
    or your life), 103
domino effect, 36, 55
Dowling, Colette, 101
    "Cinderella complex", 100
Dupuy, F., 26
Durkheim, Emile, 135

economic dependence, 62, 103
economic independence *see*
    financial independence
economic power, xi, 11, 89
economic revolution, 99
economic security, 85, 145
education system, 1, 3–4, 8, 30, 107,
    136–137
    and creation of human capital,
    31–32
    and low self-esteem, 69–70,
    102–103
egalitarians, 88, 135, 144–145,
    146
egoism, 76
emotional bonds, 38, 55, 131,
    146
emotional development, xiv, 36,
    113, 137
emotional intelligence, 2, 3, 124,
    146
    professional performance, 1

emotional maturity, 23, 29, 50, 64, 69, 66
  and frustration, 24, 27, 51
  goals and responsibilities, 39–40, 65
  and self-confidence, 124
emotional nourishment, 127, 134
emotional overflow, 49, 50, 124, 134
emotional paradigms, 2
emotional security, 85, 145
emotions, 4, 69, 77, 90, 100, 112, 119, 123, 124, 130, 131, 145, 147
  of couples, 137
  of men, 82, 84, 126, 127, 144–145
  of women, 38–40, 134, 135, 139, 146
empathy, 33, 124
employees, 26, 38–39, 93, 99, 120, 123, 125, 129 *see also* workers
  liberating people's potential, 32, 34–35, 118
  personal and professional worlds of, 135
employment discontinuity, 2, 9, 19–20, 43
  motherhood, 2, 34–35
  virtual teams, 131–132
equality/inequality, xi, xiii, xv, 4, 24, 61, 72, 89, 93, 100, 109, 116, 144
  of opportunities, 8–9
  in pay, 9, 15, 116
  of power to choose, 65, 68
  for women, 141–142
eras, 21, 99, 120, 124, 130 *see also* post-patriarchal era
  disappearing rigidities of, 127
  human development, 20
  knowledge-based society, 128
Erikson, Erik, 42, 132
  Childhood and Society, 42
ethics, 18, 28, 67, 85, 102
European communities, 20, 49, 109, 115

Eurosport, 13
evaluation/devaluation, 26, 27, 139, 147
expatriations, 21, 27, 29
expectations, 2, 3, 15, 43, 52, 79, 118, 132, 144–145, 148 *see also* social expectations
  self-esteem and, 9, 75–76
  of women, 15, 43, 118, 143
external factors, 2, 55, 75

Fabius, Laurent, 52
family, 1, 3–4, 9–10, 28, 35–36, 42, 49, 78–79, 101–104, 119, 122, 136–139, 145
  dislocation of, 20–21
  mandates of, 105–113
  and mental paradigms, 69–72
family circles, 118, 128
family life, 10, 33, 46, 132, 141
family messages, 69, 86, 112, 133
family role models, 3, 9, 86, 53–54, 63, 86, 133–135 *see also* mother figure; father figure
  and ambition, 117
  maternal, 30, 35–36, 106, 142
  paternal, 35–36, 76–77, 86, 88, 107, 122, 140, 145–146, 147
family socialization, 133–135
father figure, 30, 36, 106, 123, 133, 140 *see also* family role models; mother figure
  mentors, 133, 140
fathers, 36, 82, 88, 96, 107, 145–146
favoritism, 8
fear and guilt *see* fears; guilt
fears, 4, 15, 55, 84, 108–109, 113, 132–134, 144, 147, 148 *see also* guilt
  and dependency, 15, 142
  domino effect of, 55
  and freedom, 125–126
  of rejection, 89–100
Fedepe (Spanish Association of Women Managers, Executives and Entrepreneurs), 14

female bosses, 45, 54, 94, 95, 97–98, 116, 147 *see also* female managers/female executives; women managers
female managers/female executives, xii, xiii, 7, 13, 14, 32, 41, 48–50, 78–79, 113, 132–133, 135–137 *see also* male managers/male executives/men; female bosses; women managers
  as equals/as superiors, 141–142
  and financial socialization, 134
  male viewpoint of, 32–36, 45–47, 51
  and motherhood, 138, 146–147
  personal life, 142–143
  and renunciation, 141
  and subordinates, 140
  and teamwork, 38–40
  at workplace, 139–141
female role models, 133, 142
female self-esteem *see* self-esteem
feminine traits, xii, xiv, 45–46, 93
feminism/feminist movements, 65, 71, 115, 134
"feminist victimism", 69, 95
Ferrando, García, 42
Ferrovial, 13
fertility, 31, 39, 43
financial freedom, 2–3, 101–128
financial independence, 2, 3, 106, 113
financial socialization, 71–72, 101–113
The First Wives Club (film), 11
Fischlmayr, Iris, 10
flexibility, 9, 18–19, 24, 55, 59–61, 124, 131–132, 147
  and emotional intelligence, 124
  at work environment, 116–117
flexible capitalism, 131
formal education, 3, 4
Forward, S., 114
freedom, 59, 84, 12, 111, 114, 125, 128, 139
Freud, Sigmund, 28, 42, 132

Friedan, Betty, xiii
  mystique of femininity, xiii
frustration, xiv, 3, 15, 26, 111, 124–125
  and emotional maturity, 24, 27, 51
  and working women, 47, 71, 72, 106, 133, 141
Fundación Thyssen, 13

gender, 1, 32, 34, 45, 54, 77, 78–79, 90–91, 102, 105, 133 *see also* gender solidarity; gender stereotypes
  and class issue, 81–82
  and conflict resolution, 61–64
  differences in identity, 27–31
  and emotional maturity, 124
gender affiliation, 63–65
gender conditioning, 111–112
gender differences, 7, 72–79, 91–93
gender differentiation, 146
gender discrimination, 116, 140, 147
"the gender earthquake" films, 11–12
gender equality *see* equality/inequality
gender roles, 52, 88
gender socialization, 30–31, 133
gender solidarity, 8, 44, 63, 71, 72, 119, 132, 133, 140, 148 *see also* gender; gender stereotypes
gender stereotypes, 32, 92, 113, 123, 126, 134, 148 *see also* gender; gender solidarity
Giddens, A., 10, 44, 45
Gilligan, C., xii, 28, 132
Gimnasio Metropolitan, 13
glass ceiling, 8, 56, 92, 106
"glass walls", 10, 159n.7
Global Estrategias, 14
globalization, 17–21, 23, 24–25, 26, 39, 46, 56, 68, 97, 130, 131
Goethe, J.W., 89
Goldsmith, Olivia, 11
  The First Wives Club (novel), 11

group discussions, xiv, 3, 4, 14, 45, 63, 70, 81, 88–89, 108, 125, 126
group dynamics, 13, 14–15
  Tavistock model, 42
group meetings, 13, 31, 33, 47, 93, 108
guilt, 4, 7–8, 84, 113–128, 143 *see also* fears

Handy, Charles, 10
happiness/unhappiness, 103, **104, 105**, 145
harmony, 46, 108, 140, 142
health, 18, 21, 25, 46–47, 54, 82, 103, 142, 144
Hegelsen, S., 115
high self-esteem, 75, 126 *see also* low self-esteem; self-esteem
higher education, 1, 124, 130
human resources, 13, 34, 39, 66, 113–114
husbands, 11, 30, 35, 49, 50, 51, 57, 59, 63, 66, 70, 78, 99, 122 *see also* partners
  sacrifice for, 71, 106, 111, 139
  support from, 35, 50, 99
hypervelocity, 49, 56, 84
  impact/effects of, 1, 25–27, 39, 43
  and technological environment/new technologies, 17–18, 130–131
  women, and 15, 56, 141

ideals, 46, 51, 55, 63, 148
identification, 20, 24, 39, 86, 107
identification models, 48, 53, 86
identity, 2–4, 15, 39, 48–49, 55–56, 63, 87, 90, 114–115, 145 *see also* identity dimensions; workplace identity
  definition of, 23
  egalitarians and traditionalists, 88–89
  and gender differences, 41–43
  and hypervelocity, 25–26, 131
  social construction of, 1, 134

identity dimensions, 23–40
  differences by gender, 27–30
  and motherhood, 31–40
immediate family, 3, 118
independence/self-reliance, 4, 46–48, 56–59, 89, 100, 113, 134
  loneliness, 31, 49–50
  of men, 143–145
  women managers and, 56, 61, 64–65, 71, 107, 126
in-depth interviews, 9, 13–14, 33, 72
India, 21, 33, 61
individuals, xii, 7, 19, 21, 87
  and development of identity of, 25, 63, 131
Infoempleo, 9, 13
  study by, 9–10
informal education, 3
informal networks, 8, 10, 78, 92
information overload, 131
inhibitions, 65, 113–128
innovation, 3, 119
insecurities, xii, 15, 47–48, 97, 124, 125, 134 *see also* security
Instituto de Empresa Alumni Association, 14
integrated manager, 42, 55–63
integrated women, 63, 64, 138
integration (work and family), 15, 20, 25, 30, 137

job rotation, 18, 19–20, 147
Jung, Carl, 42, 132

Kellogg School of Management, 110
Kets de Vries, M., 42
knowledge workers, 120

Laschever, S., 109
Le Play, F., 132
leadership, 38–39, 97, 116, 117–118, 145, 146
Levinson, D., 42, 132
life cycle, 1–3, 25–26, 83, 132–139, 144, 148
  and ambition, 115–119, 121–122

and financial socialization,
105–112
and gender differences, 72–79,
115
and middle age, 75–76
theories on, 41–42
turning point of motherhood in,
31–35, 36–37, 43–44
limitations, 4, 25, 28, 43, 47, 78, 85,
161n.58
internal/external, 148
woman's awareness of her own,
50
limits, 1, 9, 24, 45, 51, 58, 94–96,
106, 139
hypervelocity pressure, 26, 43, 49,
130
time management, 37–40, 68–69
women, 30–31, 37–39, 58, 66–67,
133, 139, 141
loneliness, 7, 29, 30, 31, 49, 54, 94,
104, 112, 139
"loss of centrality", 144, 147
low self-esteem, 2, 69, 71–72,
83–84, 111, 115, 119, 122,
148 *see also* high self-esteem;
self-esteem

male culture, 8, 134, 136
male managers/male
executives/men, 45, 46, 52–55,
70, 76–79, 82–87, 90–92,
112–113, 115, 125, 127, 135,
144 *see also* female
managers/female executives;
women managers
and ambition, 93–94
and fatherhood, 88, 145–146
and masculinity, 88, 137, 144
and motherhood, 32–36,
145–146, 148
and time management, 68–69
view of female/women managers,
87–100, 147–148
view of themselves, 81–88
women as equals, 89, 141–143,
146

male menopause, 144
managing styles, 12, 34, 43, 94,
117–118, 119, 120–128,
141–142
Mapfre, 13
masculinity, 88, 137, 144
mass culture, 44, 48
material goods, 1, 2, 15, 103, 112
material provider, 135, 144
maturity, 3, 39, 42, 83
menopause, 27, 39, 58, 60, 62
see also male menopause
mental paradigms, 2
mentoring, 10, 58, 92, 123, 125,
135, 140, 147–148
benevolent differentiation, 146
father's influence, 107, 122,
133
and insider information, 92
Merck Sharp and Dohme, 13
mergers and acquisitions, 21, 84,
131
Merkel, Angela, 45
middle age, 18, 42, 63, 75, 85, 132
midlife crisis, 57, 84, 144
Miguélez, F., 42
Mill, John Stuart, xii
mind, 38, 51, 77, 108
Mintzberg, H., 117
money, xii, 2, 101–113
Moraleda, Amparo, xii
Moss Kanter, R., 7
Men and Women of the Corporation,
7
tokenism theory, 94
mother figure, 30, 51, 53–54, 61,
134 *see also* family role models;
father figure
motherhood, xiii, xiv, 2, 3–4, 41–52,
87–88, 133, 137, 141–142
and ambition and independence,
55–63
career advancement/development
and, 96, 116, 127, 135–136,
138, 146–148
multiple management skills of,
36–40

motherhood – *continued*
  and pressures on daughters, 53–54
  turning point of, 31–35, 74–75
  and women managers, 23–30

negotiation, 3, 25, 30–31, 78, 92–93,
  106, 112–113, 121, 136, 141,
  143, 147
  and paternal influence, 107–108
  process of, 54–55
  of wages, 109–111, 134
networks, 1, 122–123, 131–132, 145,
  148
  access to upper management
    positions, 2
  higher education requirement,
    136
  social spaces, 142–143
new capitalism, 119, 162
new technologies, 10, 18, 20, 59, 67,
  99
nonverbal communication, 51
nurturing, 28, 123

occupational mobility, 92
older women, 45, 46, 57, 70, 84,
  133, 139, 147
organizational behavior, 56, 72
organizational environment,
  18–21
organizational hierarchy, 8, 10
organizational models, 7–8
  hegemonic, 27
other people's games, 48, 133 *see
  also* "ball metaphor"
outsourcing, 19, 21

Parsons, Talcott, xii, 135
participation, 3, 13, 20, 33, 88, 96,
  139, 145–146
partners, xiii, 3–4, 10, 40, 87, 101,
  102, 106, 112, 114, 125,
  137–139, 143, 144 *see also*
  husbands
  and bonds, 34–35, 62, 98–99, 111,
    143
  and divorce, 137

and women's multidimensional
  guilt, 37–38, 54
patriarchal society, 33, 52, 71–72,
  88, 89, 92–100, 134
people management, 38–40
people's potential, 30, 34–35, 118,
  119, 121
performance/professional
  performance, 1, 2, 3, 8
Perrow, Charles, 42
perseverance, 24, 66, 69, 111
personal ambitions, 3
personal choices, 45, 67–68, 73–74
personal development, xiv, xv, 2,
  123, 129, 142, 145
personality, 11–12, 27, 29, 39, 42,
  43, 56, 64, 105, 132, 160n.23
  emotional aspect of, 124–125
  ethics of character, 85–86
  flexible attitude, 60–61
  male perceptions of female bosses,
    97–98
Piñuel, I., 25
planning, 50, 66, 68, 142
positions of power, 45, 107
post-patriarchal era, 100, 125, 137
  see also eras
power (and authority), 2, 7, 12, 46,
  89–92, 103, 104–105, 115,
  145
  and economic circles, 102, 144
  networks and support groups, 11,
    93–94, 123, 131
  and new woman, 47–48, 56, 65,
    68–69, 121, 140, 146
power games, 46
pregnancy, 35, 62, 97, 99, 121, 135,
  138
pressures, 7–8, 15, 42, 51, 62, 91, 98,
  110, 142
  of beauty myth, 56, 132–133
  and competitive managers, 43–45
  for daughters, 53–54
  of hypervelocity, 43, 17–21, 68–69
  and stereotypes, 142, 148
priorities, 15, 24, 39, 46, 51
  by men, 126–128, 144–145

motherhood and, 86–87,
132–133, 138
at stages of life cycle, 25–26, 36,
48–49, 115–116
by women managers, 37–40, 66,
119–120, 121, 123, 141
proactive attitude, 54, 73, 142
professional development, xiv, 2–3,
63–64, 74, 111, 137
and mentoring processes, 10
and motherhood, 55–56, 87
search for a strategy for, 75
see also career development
professional performance, 2, 3, 8,
26, 33, 48, 118
professional take-off, 43, 55
professional socialization, 1, 3, 90,
143
promotions, 1, 3, 10–11, 43, 66,
117, 125, 140
and mentor figures, 58, 121–122
possibilities, 1, 57, 121
training in management skills
and, 136

"queen bee"
phenomenon/syndrome, 8, 94,
135
questionnaire, 4, 14, 149–152

readjustments, 4, 127, 128
reconciliation (of work and family),
xiii, 1, 2, 10, 15, 20, 30, 34,
43–44, 57, 68, 131–132, 137,
141
and male managers, 78–79
need for support at all levels,
35–36
and working women, 41–42, 116,
119, 121–122, 133, 136
relationships, 4, 9, 23–24, 28, 38,
53, 72, 78, 109, 134
depersonalized, 20
interrelationships, 42, 52
material things and, 107
money and, 113–128
new woman and, 61, 97–98, 102

in technological environment,
17–21
renunciation, xiv, 1, 15, 46, 47–48,
141
reproduction, 3, 32, 119–120
Requena Santos, F., 42
research/qualitative methodology
approach, 3–5, 13–15, 149–156
responsibility, xii, xiii, 4, 34, 63, 70,
92, 137
Rifkin, J., 17, 130
risks, 9, 15, 19, 29, 50, 58, 64, 67,
130, 133
aversion, 15, 58
experience of motherhood and,
56–57
high self-esteem and, 75–76
self-confidence and, 9, 20
rivalry, 46, 85, 96, 130, 134
Robert Allen-Horton, 14
Robin, V.
"La bolsa o la vida" (Your purse or
your life), 103
role models, xii–xiii, 1, 15, 64, 75,
86, 106, 117
family socialization, 132–135
roles, 4, 51, 52, 65, 78, 111–112,
126, 128, 143
diversifying, 83–84, 88
of men, 83, 96, 100, 124–125,
145, 146, 147
multiplicity of women's, 3,
36–40, 46, 48, 49, 89, 90, 106,
134
traditional, 9–10, 63, 97, 99, 145
Royal, Ségoléne, 45, 52, 102

sacrifices, xiv, 33, 48, 57, 68, 70, 71,
99, 109–110, 141
Sánchez Apellániz, Mercedes, 9
Sarrió, M., 8, 52
"queen bee" phenomenon, 8
security, 70–71, 75, 76, 110–111,
125, 131 *see also* insecurities
self image, 4, 56, 81–100
self perception *see* self image
self-awareness, 63, 65, 83, 102, 110

self-confidence, 9, 83–84, 111, 125, 126
self-esteem, 2, 3, 9, 75–76 *see also* high self-esteem; low self-esteem
selfishness, 3, 29, 108, 136, 142, 145
selflessness, xii, 3, 101–102, 108, 113, 123 *see also* altruism
self-sufficiency, 15, 102, 134
Sennett, R., 20, 25, 119, 121, 131
separation (and attachment), 28, 29
sexual harassment/sexist culture, 52, 90
sexual objects, 44, 45, 140
sexuality, 52, 53, 56, 62, 84, 96
Sheehy, G., 42, 91, 100
sibling relationships, 3
Simmel, G., 132, 134
"social Darwinism", 43, 140
social expectations, 3, 79, 148
social pressure, 23, 44, 99, 136–137
social recognition, 76
social responsibility, 18, 33, 147
socialization, 4, 27, 52–53, 58, 61, 133–138
  and material matters, 76
  and men, 71–72, 77, 85–86, 90, 115, 127, 143–145
  and women, 101, 124, 139–142
society, xii, xv, 25, 29–32, 35, 39, 44, 46, 49, 54, 63, 88, 108, 109, 116–117, 120, 128, 160n.23
  effects of short-term views of, 84–85, 119, 131
  and family bond, 64–65
  key elements in, 119
  living with guilt, 143
  and material compensation, 76
  taboos of, 103
sociology of organizations, xi–xii, 10, 41–42, 132
spaces, 60, 62, 142–143, 145
Spain, xi, xii, 7, 29, 36, 37, 67, 68, 73, 78, 81, 98, 121, 104
  Gender Equality Law, xi
speed/pace, 15, 17–19, 25, 26, 39, 96, 99, 122, 130, 131

springboards, 101–105, 111, 139
strategic planning, 11, 142
strategies, 46, 63, 68, 84, 127, 133
  career, 73–75, 136
  heading corporations, 86–87, 129
  of temporary renunciation, 108
Strauss, L., 160n.23
Streep, Meryl, 12
subordinates, 4, 125, 134, 140, 147–148
support groups (for women), 11, 72

teamwork, xiv, 38–40, 130
technological dependence, 19
technological environment, 17–18
tension (fears and insecurity), 15, 18–19, 21, 39, 44, 115, 123, 140
Thelma and Louise (film), 11
  "the gender earthquake", 11
time management, 39, 68–69, 136
"tired woman's syndrome", 38
Tobio, C., 50
Touraine, A., 10, 44, 97
traditionalism, 9, 10, 26, 88, 97, 101, 137, 144
  of men, 26, 89
  view of money, 105–113
  of women, 76, 117–128
training, 9, 15, 74, 94–95, 105, 126, 135, 136
  benefits of, 26, 62, 115, 116
  and maternal influence, 106–107
transformation, 23, 86, 110, 146
transformational leadership, **118**

uncertainty, 19, 20, 60, 86
unconditional love, 71, 113
United States, 7, 8, 9, 18, 45, 73, 117, 122
Universia, 13
upper management, 1, 2, 3–4, 7, 9–10, 13, 15, 24, 140, 141, 94–95, 117, 142, 148
  behavior of, 41–42
  description of, 129

obstacles on path to, 92–93, 96,
122
women in, 48, 52–53, 87, 101–103
upper management positions, xi, 1, 3,
4, 7, 13, 37, 42, 87, 117, 122, 129
poor presence of women in, xiv,
9–10
"queen bee" phenomenon, 8
tokenism in, 7, 94, 141

Valian, Virginia, 110
"Why so slow in the advancement
of women", 110
values, 9, 18, 20, 33–34, 49, 85–86,
88, 99, 102, 105, 112
and inhibitions, 113–128
at stages of life cycle, 36
vulnerability, 26–27, 44–45, 69, 71,
88, 95
"corporate beauty" awards, 44–45

Washington Quality Group, 14
wealth, 11, 12, 31, 114
Weber, Marianne, 135
Wolf, N., 29, 42, 44
women managers, xiii, xv, 1, 2, 4,
13, 23–40, 41–42, 86, 136 *see
also* male managers/male
executives/men; female
managers/female executives
attitudes of, 24–27
background to, 8–12
gender differences and, 72–79
male standpoint of, 87–100

types of
competitive manager, 43–54
integrated manager, 55–63
proactive manager, 64–68
reactive manager, 69–71
women's professional advancement
see career development
women's self-esteem *see* self-esteem
work relations, 3, 41, **120**, 140
workers, 2, 9–10, 17–18, 26, 46, 58,
120–121 *see also* employees
loss of identity of, 131–132
pressures upon, 19–21
working hours, 9, 18–19, 32, 68
working life, 131, 132–133
workplace identity, 19, 39, 128
see also identity; identity
dimensions
loss of, 131–132
organizational models of, 7–8,
25
women's gender-oriented role in,
7–8, 133
workplace socialization, 3
World Conference on Women
(Beijing, 1995), xi

younger generations, 36, 85, 107,
137
younger women, xiii–xiv, 15, 88, 99,
137, 139, 141, 143
accountable outlook of, 102
ambitions of, 43
competitiveness of, 46, 60–61

FI-P17